THE BEST OF
REMINISCE

REMINISCE.

We are committed to both the quality
of our products and the service we
provide to our customers. We value
your comments, so please feel free
to contact us at TMBBookTeam@
TrustedMediaBrands.com.

For more *Reminisce* products and
information, visit our website:
www.reminisce.com

Printed in China
10 9 8 7 6 5 4 3 2 1

Text, photography and illustrations for
The Best of Reminisce 2023 are based
on articles previously published in
Reminisce magazine.

CONTENTS

SMILES AND BARE FEET
We had shoes for church. The rest of that summer in 1951, it was toes out. I'm second from right. With me are Billy Smith, Tommy Edwards, Johnny Smith and Eddie Godsell.
JOHN CULP SR. • WEST COLUMBIA, SC

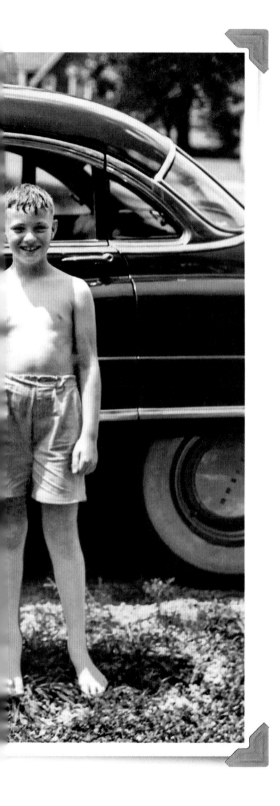

Getting together with the neighborhood kids for some barefoot summer fun is just one of the happy moments depicted in this new keepsake collection of nostalgic stories and photos from the previous year of *Reminisce*.

The Best of Reminisce features many other recollections of growing up, along with memories of family fun and stories of that fluttering butterfly feeling that can lead up to a lifetime of love and marriage.

Enjoy a glimpse at once-popular products and fashions, such as sofa beds, Polaroid cameras and Farrah Fawcett's feather-cut hairdo.

Read accounts of hardworking Americans and what inspired them, as well as touching words on and from those who served our country during times of conflict. Also here are memories of vintage autos (with a timeline on the popular Cadillac), chance encounters with stars and loving tributes to old songs that will have you digging out your old records.

We hope you find comfort, joy and so much more as you journey back in time with *The Best of Reminisce*.

THE EDITORS OF *REMINISCE* MAGAZINE

CHAPTER 1

GROWING UP

Getting a first library card, playing ball and friendly smiles bring back fond memories of youth.

Warm Smiles

The weather turned bright and beautiful after a snowstorm
one winter's day in 1966, and our kids Bruce, Linda and twins
Billy and Susan took advantage of it. This was taken in front
of our home in Hauppauge, New York, on Long Island.

ODETTE LANDERS · FORT PIERCE, FL

Browsing shelves at the library for the first time as an independent reader is a delight few forget.

Key to the Kingdom

Unlocking the code to a world of knowledge.

———

The exact year escapes me, although I guess it was probably 1958 or 1959, but I do know that I was still in elementary school when I learned the Dewey Decimal System. Mostly, I remember the wonderful feeling of accomplishment, of feeling smart and confident. Any book could be located by title, author or subject. Every book had an address on a shelf.

I had mastered the skill I needed to learn more about anything and everything, not just what was in our textbooks. This was like discovering a pirate's map!

It sparked an awakening of curiosity about all things. Our neighborhood library was one of the little brick Andrew Carnegie buildings scattered across the United States. It was only a few blocks from my family's house in the quiet neighborhood of Lester Park in Duluth, Minnesota.

After getting my very own library card, I spent an entire summer reading whatever subjects I could think up next. There were books on magic tricks and puppetry, books of jokes, riddles and puns, science books that told how things work, and something new to me—science fiction.

I remember in particular a green clothbound book of the masterworks of Jules Verne, including *The Mysterious Island*, *Twenty Thousand Leagues Under the Sea*, *From the Earth to the Moon*, *A Journey to the Center of the Earth* and more.

I couldn't get enough of this genre. I used my newfound knowledge of the card catalog to find H.G. Wells and many other writers.

Each time, I checked out an armful of books on assorted subjects. I think the maximum allowed was five books, and they had to be back in two weeks. A librarian would remove the book card from its pocket inside the front cover, stamp the card and file it, and then stamp the book's due date on a slip of paper glued next to the pocket.

I always walked to the library instead of riding my bike, as it didn't have a basket or saddlebags to carry all my books home.

I dutifully returned all of my booty on time. I like to think it was because I was being a good citizen—and I was—but mostly it was because I wouldn't be able to pay the 10-cents-a-day fine for overdue books. Or worse, have my library card revoked.

I have to smile whenever I read about someone who, after many years, returns a forgotten book to a library, along with a check for hundreds—sometimes thousands—of dollars and a note of apology for the late return.

That could very easily have been me returning an old green clothbound book that first transfixed an 11-year-old boy.

RANDOLPH CARL HALVERSON
ENGLEWOOD, CO

I remember in particular a green clothbound book of the masterworks of Jules Verne.

Cool grown-up Bill Thomas made summer fun for Emily, Eileen, Bruce and Mark in 1956.

Bothering Bill

Welsh grad student shakes up kids' world.

Our grandfather was a famous lawyer in China who fled when the Communists took over in 1949. We visited him every summer in Princeton, New Jersey. He—disgruntled, without meaningful work and perhaps being a typical Chinese grandfather—sat on his sun porch all day, reading and never talking to us.

His second wife, who was younger than my mom, had been a "dancing girl" in China. She was kind to us, but we couldn't speak Chinese and she couldn't speak English. That left us kids—ages 5, 6, 7 and 9—with only one another on those summer visits from our home in Detroit, Michigan.

One evening, we went outside to catch fireflies. My sister and I watched surprised as our brothers played and wrestled on the lawn with Bill, a Princeton Ph.D. student from Wales who rented our grandfather's basement. In the Chinese world, elders didn't play with children and roughhousing was out of the question!

Bill became our favorite friend. We bothered him whenever we could: He made us milkshakes, let us help him change the tires on his old car and introduced us to his friends from Europe. When we went home, he wrote us kind letters, encouraging us to study hard and play hard. We named our pet turtle Bill.

The summer came when Bill finished his degree and returned home. I was 12. We moved to Seattle, and Bill still wrote us, but less often. We felt we had lost him.

Recently I received a program from a memorial service. I didn't recognize the white-haired man in the photo, but I knew the name—William Thomas. Bill's son Des had found my address and sent it.

As a result, I gained two new friends: Des, and Bill's wife, Mary, who lives in England. We keep in touch, and I like to think our friendship began on a soft summer evening more than 60 years ago when I first met Bill.

EILEEN YOUNG · SEATTLE, WA

The Old House in Rusk

Brothers navigate the gullies of East Texas.

My grandparents' house in Rusk, Texas, stood at the end of a red dirt road on the edge of town. Behind the house was a hill—we called it a mountain—covered with tall East Texas pines. Inside was a huge red brick fireplace with a broad hearth.

The old house was covered in weathered gray clapboard and had a wide porch that ran across the front and around one side. During several memorable months we spent with my grandparents in 1951, my older brother, Eddie, and I passed hours there, playing in the cool, dry dirt under the porch. Afterward, we'd take a bath in a big black tub in the front yard and wait for Dad to come home, driving the truck that was used for hauling pulpwood. Sometimes he would bring us a Grapette soda, right from the bottling company in town.

A deep ditch ran along the road in front of the house. Every time it rained, water poured down the hill, eroding the gully a little more—and it seemed that in time the whole road would be washed away. The bottom of the ditch was thick with brush, and I had a terrible fear of sliding in and landing on a timber rattlesnake. We called them canebrake rattlers, and Eddie said they were everywhere. He told me he'd seen one down in the brush, "sitting up on its hind legs and looking at me." I believed him.

Eddie also told me to hit the dirt every time a red airplane flew over, because that was a Japanese aircraft. Fortunately, we hardly ever saw red planes, and I realized later that by the '50s we were fairly safe from attack.

Many years later, I visited the site where the house had stood. The dirt was still red, and the pine trees were still tall. But the hill behind the house was, after all, just a hill. The fireplace and hearth that remained weren't as huge as I had remembered.

And the gully that seemed as if it would swallow the road? It was just a shallow wash with tall weeds—although I heard my own little boy telling his brother to stay away from the deep ditch. I wondered if he told him there were snakes down there.

STEVE TUNNELL · SOMERVILLE, TX

Steve with his big brother, Eddie, in 1951.

Caught on the Run

There wasn't time for a cover-up.

Playsuits were the latest fashion in 1943 when I was 11. The style consisted of a one-piece blouse and shorts combo, with a button-up-the-front skirt to cover up the shorts.

One warm day in Princeton, Indiana, I pleaded with my mother to let me wear my playsuit to school. She gave in after some discussion, but insisted that I not, under any circumstance, remove the skirt. I promised.

Unbeknownst to me, Dad left work early that day so my parents could surprise me with a new bike. He put it in the basement where I would find it after school, then my parents sat down to wait for me to get home.

Because of some small offense, I had to stay after school briefly that day. The usual time for my arrival home came and went, and Mother became concerned. She sent Dad in the car to meet me.

Meanwhile, I was coming home, and realizing I was late, I started to run. Running without the skirt was faster, so I took it off. Imagine my surprise when I saw Dad driving toward me as I ran in shorts, carrying that skirt! With hardly a word, I got in the car and we drove home.

My parents may have had second thoughts about giving me their gift. Nevertheless, we three went down to the basement and there it was—a new green Schwinn, with a basket for my dog, CeeFee Jo. Then we were all smiles—Mother may have had a tear in her eye. No bike has ever been as beautiful as that one.

JOAN BARTON · EVANSVILLE, IN

Joan loved pedaling around town with CeeFee Jo in the basket.

Frank and Helen with sons Jerry and Larry are dressed in their Easter best in 1946.

Choose Your Weapon Wisely

Boys bring all-natural arsenal into play in pasture duel.

My brother, Jerry, and I were more than a bit naughty. We enjoyed a colorful, adventuresome childhood with our long-suffering mother, Helen, and our father, Frank, called Zeke, whose hobby was hunting small game and preserving their pelts in our garage.

Jerry was younger than I, and we were baptized together in 1949 at the Chelsea Baptist Church in Kansas City, Kansas. But we didn't change our frisky ways for the better until we got older.

We loved trips to our uncle's farm outside of Kansas City. Uncle Robert had a mob of chickens and a milk cow, Bessie. Tall weeds grew in Bessie's pasture—when they became dry and brittle, they made excellent spears for two battling brothers.

One day, my side of the pasture was out of the usual weapons. At first I avoided Bessie's droppings, which littered the field. But then I noticed that some of the lighter-colored patties seemed to be dry. I gingerly picked up one of the disks—it smelled a bit like dried grass.

I launched my "Frisbee" and Jerry recognized the missile for what it was. To retaliate, he sought a patty of his own. But having done no research, he didn't understand that not all cow pies are alike. He picked up the first one available, which was fresh. His fingers sank into the mess and he ran for the stream at the bottom of the hill, screaming for our mother all the way.

LARRY THOMAS · HUMBLE, TX

Dianne, holding a *TV Guide*, and Deborah, far right, helped one another through an adolescent rite of passage.

On the Path to Womanhood

Girls pass first test of maturity with flying colors.

G awky and a math dullard in the mid-1960s, I towered over the petite, charming Miss Jackson, who wore stylish pencil skirts and knew everything there was to know about math. All of us girls wanted to be like her when we grew up.

The other sixth grade teacher, Mr. Jacobson, came to our classroom during his free periods, and we decided he was her boyfriend. She pretended not to notice, but it seemed her lessons had more oomph when he was observing.

On the playground, older girls had told us of an educational movie about a girl named Becky and her path to womanhood. We'd also heard that the boys had their own version of a film on growing up. We all waited for our turn for The Talk with nervous anticipation.

When film day came, the boys noisily pushed their way into Mr. Jacobson's room. The girls in Miss Jackson's room were quieter, whispering together. My friend Dianne Lewis and I sat side by side for emotional support.

Miss Jackson's voice quavered as she introduced the film and started the projector. Then she fled to the back of the room.

Even though we'd discussed this film among ourselves, we were not prepared for the frank explanations by the chirpy narrator. Mortified, we looked at the floor. Miss Jackson strode to the front of the darkened classroom. "Girls, the information is up here, it's not on the floor."

Timidly we looked up to where our teacher stood in front of the screen. Bright illustrations of Becky's journey were projected onto Miss Jackson's sweater. She stayed put, trying to get our attention while the subject of the film switched to material about the boys. We could see that they too were marching toward maturity. This was too much for Miss Jackson, who was clearly as embarrassed as we were. She was only about 25 at the time and in her first teaching job.

Fred stands with older sister Marion.

Sensing Miss Jackson's discomfort, Dianne got up and fiddled with the projector until it clicked off. Miss Jackson sat down at her desk. "Ladies, I apologize. I should have previewed the film. I was nervous about today, but I should have realized you might be nervous as well."

Now what? No teacher had ever apologized to us before and we weren't sure what to do. But our newly attained maturity came to the rescue. Someone in the front row got up and gave Miss Jackson a hug. Then, one by one, we all expressed our sympathy and understanding for the awkward situation.

We never finished the film about Becky. But, as a class, we read and discussed some of the material in the pink Kimberly-Clark pamphlets that Miss Jackson handed out.

A few days later, Miss Jackson sent each girl an elegantly handwritten note, apologizing for causing us embarrassment and inviting us to talk to her if we wanted to. After that, I was positive I wanted to be exactly like Miss Jackson—she's one of the reasons I became a teacher.

And we were right about one thing: She married Mr. Jacobson the next year.

DEBORAH NORDLIE · CORONADO, CA

NEWSPAPERS TOLD HIM WHEN TO GO TO THE MOVIES

EVERY TWO WEEKS IN THE EARLY 1940s—after I finished my cornflakes at breakfast—Mom gave me 25 cents and two streetcar tickets. She wanted me out of the house so she could scrub the kitchen floor. Experience taught me that when newspapers were scattered all over the floor, I was supposed to keep out so I didn't track dirt on the linoleum.

I went to the movies. The children's amateur hour was first, then out went the lights and *Movietone News* about the war came on. After that were *Looney Tunes* cartoons and then two cowboy shows, with actors such as Gene Autry and Hopalong Cassidy. Being cowboy movies, the outcome was fairly certain. Before the second one wrapped up, boredom usually set in.

When I got back home, the newspapers were gone, the floor was scrubbed and my father was home from work. After a long day of watching movies, I was hungry, tired and ready for bed.

FRED E. ZOERB · IRWIN, PA

Signatures in Time

Mom's autograph book offers a glimpse of student life.

Looking through my mom's things after her death, I came across a treasure: a small, green leather-bound autograph book full of signatures of classmates from her junior high years. Autograph books have been around a long time—I had a plastic-bound one in the 1960s—but I rarely see them nowadays. Eventually, yearbooks were the preferred way to sign messages for classmates.

My mother's provides a wonderful summary of her early years, the history of the times and a glimpse of her friends.

My mom, Kaye Duncan, was 15 when her mother gave her the autograph book on Valentine's Day 1937. Mom was attending Morey Junior High School in Denver and was vice president of her class. From references in the entries, I learned that Mom enjoyed tennis, golf, ice skating and sleigh riding. Her book also contains popular quotations from the time written down by her school chums. Some of the sayings are cute, others are sweet and a few are downright corny. Mom always had a sense of humor and it shows throughout the book. Most entries are written in fountain pen.

I am so happy to have found this memento of my mother's younger days. I love seeing how her personality developed into the beautiful person she became.

JULIE MANN · CENTENNIAL, CO

Julie's mother, Kaye Duncan, in the sweater top, kept an autograph book of her time at Morey Junior High in Denver.

Mrs. Shelt gave her first graders the lifetime pleasure of reading. Anna is at far left in the second row.

Words to Live By

Remember when everything was letter-perfect?

All the classroom doors were open and the halls of Washington Elementary School in Tiffin, Ohio, rang as every child, first grade through sixth, drilled their sound sticks. Sound sticks were narrow paper strips with consonants and their sounds on one side, and the vowels—long, short and special—on the other.

"B says *buh, buh, buh*. C says *cuh, cuh, cuh*."

In the fall of 1955, I was a happy first grader with beautiful Mrs. Shelt as my teacher. I can still see her in her 1950s-style narrow-waisted, full-skirted dress, standing at the blackboard, pointer in hand.

"*Mmm-o-th*," she said. She smiled. "Use your sounds. Who can read this word?"

I waved my hand wildly. I had figured it out! That was the magic moment when it all made sense and I became a reader.

"Yes, Anna Jean?"

And I answered, "Mother!"

Right then and there, I decided to become a first grade teacher. I wanted to be able to share the precious gift of reading.

I did become a teacher, spending 18 years teaching first graders, two years teaching language arts to fifth graders and 10 years as a librarian—all at what is now Woodridge Elementary School in Cuyahoga Falls, Ohio. I have many fond memories of bringing children and books together.

Over the years, reading remained a major part of my life. I always have a book on my nightstand. Books have taken me to foreign lands and long-ago times, and introduced me to amazing people both real and fictional. I shared in their joys and sorrows and filled many hours with the pleasures of reading. I owe Mrs. Shelt my deepest gratitude.

ANNA J. WADSWORTH · BRECKSVILLE, OH

A MEAL READY TO EAT

Kids can make a self-serve breakfast with a variety of cereal options.

« 1949

Cereal in a Snap

Kellogg's Rice Krispies debuted in 1928 with the slogan "Help Yourself to Health," an apparent early nod to cold cereal as a quick answer to sudden hunger. This ad touts that Krispies are "tops with school kids," but the tagline "Mother Knows Kellogg's Best" suggests that in 1949, a parent puts the kids' breakfast on the table.

1962 »

The Skinny on Marketing

It was advertisers, tasked in 1944 with persuading us to eat the wheat-and-barley cereal called Grape-Nuts, who came up with the adage "breakfast is the most important meal of the day." In the '60s, Grape-Nuts became associated with healthy eating and dieting.

You can't keep a good man down.

"The **best** to you each morning"

Best liked (*World's favorite*)
Best flavor (*Kellogg's secret*)
Worst to run out of (*"Pick up a spare," says Yogi Bear*)

Kellogg's

CORN FLAKES

1962 | Why Wait for Mom?

By 1962, cereal is well established as a meal kids can prepare for themselves. Corn Flakes, a venerable Kellogg's product introduced in 1894, got its colorful rooster on the box in 1958. Today, Cornelius is one of corporate America's most recognizable characters.

TO BE A KID AGAIN

MAY DAY BIRTHDAY

My mother always put up a maypole for my May 1 birthday. In 1950 or '51, when I was 6 or 7, I invited my friends from school in Willmar. My sister Julie is the tall girl at the back; I'm the one in the striped shirt at the head of the table.

STEPHEN SCHNEIDER
JORDAN, MN

BEST DRESS

My parents lived in a duplex, and my grandparents lived on the other side of us. They watched me while my parents went to work in Los Angeles, California. Here I am in 1948, wearing my favorite velvet dress.

MARGE HOLLEY • FILER, ID

GRANDMA'S KITCHEN

Grandma Custer made biscuits and the best-smelling sugar cookies in her kitchen in Mendon, Ohio, in the mid-'50s. Granddad Custer hid his whiskey in the barn because Grandma didn't allow liquor of any kind. Even rum cake at Christmas was banned.

BOB DUSTMAN • AUBURN HILLS, MI

SOLDIER SISTERS

Every Sunday, my mother, Lillian, my sister, Betty, and I rode the bus to Grandmother Wilbanks' house for dinner. Dad and his two brothers were in the Army. One Sunday when we were all at Grandma's house, my uncles were ordered back to base immediately because the Japanese had bombed Pearl Harbor. Betty and I didn't understand what had happened, but we saw that the adults were shocked. This picture of us in our soldier suits was taken in 1942, when I was 7 and Betty was 5.

BARBARA W. HARRIS · NEWNAN, GA

Similar to Sandra's high school jackknife diving test, this diver seems to pull off the challenging dive.

Headfirst into the Unknown

Never underestimate the power of desperate thinking.

———

The dreaded day of our diving test in my Monday morning high school physical education class was here. Our parents thought we were privileged to have an Olympic-size swimming pool at the school. My mom emphasized that the schools in Massachusetts were the best in the country, and luxuries like the pool were proof. But I wasn't so sure.

Not only was I terribly shy in regular classes and sat in the back of the room so I'd not be called upon to read, each Monday I would work my way to the back of the line forming at the diving board so I would not have to practice the dives.

My blood ran cold when the teacher announced we would be graded for our final on the most difficult dive—the jackknife. I trembled as the line to the awful diving board shortened. As I watched, each student seemed to perform the challenging dive effortlessly, and shortly I would have to attempt something I'd never even practiced before.

Then I remembered someone telling me that when you picture yourself doing a skill over and over, it's just as effective as physically practicing that skill. So I watched carefully as each girl jumped at the end of the board once, added a jump for height, folded her body in half to reach for her toes, and finally straightened out like an arrow for entry into the water. I think I was actually in a state of shock, because all of a sudden I saw these four steps as doable.

Then it was my turn. With my heart pounding and knowing I was going to be embarrassed beyond belief, I walked down the board, jumped once and then again to get height, folded for the toe reach, and stretched out just as I had pictured in my mind, entering the water straight as an arrow.

I received a perfect grade on my dive that day and an A for the course.

It was awesome to think that I had just learned my first dive, while at the same time, I suspected it would be my last. Now, over 50 years later, I'm convinced of it.

SANDRA NIMS EUBANKS · MOBILE, AL

I think I was actually in a state of shock, because all of a sudden I saw these four steps as doable.

They Had Game

Everyone caught the fever for neighborhood pickup.

S omething was special about our working-class Evansville neighborhood in the 1950s—baseball. It proved to be more lasting than many fads of the era, and it forged a bond among the kids living near the viaduct on the city's north side.

On hazy, humid summer evenings, we played pickup ballgames in various backyards and neighborhood lots. We weren't especially steeped in a lot of organization, and the rules were pretty simple: Three strikes, you're out; flyball caught, you're out; tagged before the base, you're out. No walks. No umpires. If you hit a fair ball, you run as fast as you can because there are no automatic doubles, triples or homers.

Hillerich & Bradsby Co., founded in 1856, makes about 2 million wood bats a year— 50,000 for the majors.

Anyone could play, boys or girls—heck, some of the girls could hit the farthest and throw the hardest. If you cheated or whined, you were banned from play, but these sins rarely occurred. We played until the sun sank and we could no longer see the ball.

Our equipment consisted of an old Louisville Slugger bat "willed" to us by an older child who went on to play Little League. We also had a couple of used softballs and a few of us were lucky enough to have gloves. When the haves were at bat, they shared with the have-nots—and among them, infielders got dibs on the gloves over the outfielders, the rationale being that the ball lost its zip after a trip through the infield, making it easier to catch or pick up bare-handed once it reached the outfield.

Bases were improvised—the clothesline post, a piece of cardboard, smashed tins fished out of the trash.

We had neither fans nor coaches. Our great plays were never publicized. Yet we loved it and played for the love of the game itself. We learned to settle our differences with little or no intervention from adults.

Each evening, we were the Mickey Mantles and Hank Aarons of Evansville, imagining thousands cheering us on.

CAROL WILL · EVANSVILLE, IN

One Incredible Dinger

That ball is outta here! Wait—where is it?

One day in the 1950s in South Jersey, my friend Arnold joined me in the backyard to blast pebbles with a chipped Louisville Slugger.

In our teenage imaginations, we were Willie Mays and Mickey Mantle at practice. Most of our home runs traveled far and high above the pines and oaks that dotted an adjacent lot.

Just as we were thinking of calling it a day, Arnold found a golf ball on the ground.

"How far do you think this will go if I connect?"

He gritted his teeth and tossed the golf ball in the air fungo-style, and then smacked it with a lusty uppercut of his Slugger.

Up, up and away it sailed. We were sure it would have cleared the roof at Yankee Stadium. We laughed hysterically and wondered where it landed. We soon found out.

We heard the wail of a siren and saw an ambulance headed in the same direction as the ball had traveled. Proceeding stealthily through the woods and across 12th Street, we came to a group of about five people standing over a figure facedown on the pavement.

When the rescue squad lifted the victim onto a stretcher, we were shocked to discover it was our friend Benny, who had been on his way to join us. Everyone was looking up into a giant maple tree for some clue as to what had felled the poor kid, who now had a lump on his forehead about the size—suspiciously—of a golf ball.

At the time, and for years after, Arnold and I were too overwhelmed by guilt and anxiety to offer the implausible, but likely accurate, explanation—that Benny had indeed been struck by a golf ball launched a block and a half away with the evident accuracy of a Scud missile.

About 25 years ago, we had Benny to dinner when he was in town visiting, and we spilled the beans. He touched the scar on his forehead, but he didn't believe us. He thought, and still thinks, that he was shagging fly balls in a sandlot when the webbing of his glove broke. This confirms that Benny was knocked cold by Arnold's whopper, with no recollection of the incident.

If Benny reads this account and learns the truth at last, Arnold and I would like to offer him our apologies and say something we should have said long ago: Fore!

WILLIAM DOMENICO · HAMMONTON, NJ

Joltin' Joe DiMaggio kisses his autographed Louisville Slugger.

Kelley, No. 3, a point guard, gets around the defense in this game in 1965.

Hoops Player Has a Good Run

Inside the locker room at the epic tournament
that became March Madness.

That autumn day in 1956, I rushed down to the locker room at Roman Catholic High School in Philadelphia to see if my name was on the list of those who had made the basketball team.

It wasn't there.

I decided right then I'd run 4 miles a day and practice as many hours as it took so that next time, I'd be in far superior condition to my competitors.

The next autumn, when I looked for my name on that list it was there.

In games, I racked up points with an arcing long-distance jump shot. I led the division in scoring and was named to the Catholic all-league team.

More importantly, at least to my pop, I got several scholarship offers to play basketball.

I chose hometown Temple University and began to work toward that pinnacle of college basketball: playing in the NCAA tournament known today as March Madness.

On March 9, 1964, my team sat in the locker room, waiting to take the court against the University of Connecticut in the first round of the tournament. My arms were covered with goose bumps as we listened to the 10,000 screaming fans.

Sadly, we lost in the most disappointing defeat of my playing days. Weeks later, I recovered my spirits, realizing what an honor and privilege it was to be one of the few college players who ever get the chance to be part of this phenomenal event.

B.G. KELLEY · PHILADELPHIA, PA

Dottie poses with lifeguards Joe Foster and John McInerney at Rehoboth Beach in 1954.

Dottie's hair is under wraps for the photo in the *Star*, far left; near left, she uncovers her stylish pageboy.

On-The-Spot Glamour Girl

Diary details Mom's day in the sun.

My mother, Dorothy, called Dottie, kept her teenage diaries wrapped in tissue in an upstairs drawer. I started reading them—lovely penmanship, creative spelling and all. From time to time I'd laugh out loud and read one to Mom.

She'd supply details about the diary entry: the boy who crashed his car into a tree because he turned to look at Mom and Mary McNeil walking down the street; her trick of talking endlessly to avoid an unwanted kiss; and babysitting, homework, phone calls, dresses and dances.

Two entries from 1954 recalled Dottie's unexpected turn as a model when she was 15. Chaperoned by a set of parents, the girls in Kappa Beta Psi sorority at Woodrow Wilson High School in Washington, D.C., drove to Rehoboth Beach, Delaware, for a two-week stay in a cottage.

The girls were keeping an eye out for boys on the beach when a lifeguard ran up, grabbed Dottie's wrist and practically dragged her to the lifeguard stand. All arms and legs at 5 feet 11 inches, she must have looked like a cartoon stumbling after him.

"Here's our girl!" he said to someone holding a camera. The man was *Washington Star* photographer Paul Schmick, who was working on a feature about lifeguards for the *Washington Star Pictorial Magazine*. He told Dottie where to stand (closer) and whom to look at (the lifeguards). He had her smile. And smile once more. Then he wrote her name in a little book and left.

After the story was published that August, Dottie's neighbor Paul Miller, a popular senior, came bolting out of his house: "I saw you! I saw you in the *Star*!"

Dottie's dad bought a dozen copies of the paper and hung a print of the photo in his office. Her practical mother asked, "Dottie, why didn't you take off your scarf and show them your hair?"

She hadn't had time to think of uncovering her auburn pageboy, which was under wraps to protect it from the sun and wind and to hide the bobby pins setting the curls she needed later. After all, it was a date night!

SUZIE SIMS-FLETCHER · ASTORIA, NY

Fred's lunker made headlines in the local paper.

Catch of a Lifetime

On the hunt for a watery monster.

A lthough I can't recall the first time my dad took me fishing, I do remember my first lunker.

It was the summer of 1950, a few months after I turned 10. My folks allowed that I was old enough to spend the summer at my grandpa's farm in Macoupin County, Illinois.

Grandpa's neighbor had a pond that had been built by the Civilian Conservation Corps in the 1930s. It had an abundance of perch. But nearby was another pond that was said to contain monster catfish. So that was where I headed with my 5-foot bean pole, which I grabbed from a pile by the garden gate.

Sitting on the pond's diving board, I was catching small perch as fast as I could drop my bait in the water. Suddenly, the cork went under, and I thought I was going to be dragged right off my seat. I jumped up, ran backward up the bank and literally dragged my catfish out of the water—while yelling at the top of my lungs.

Grandpa thought I was drowning. He and the rest of the household took off running toward the pond.

We met halfway in the garden. But when I raised my pole to show off my prize, the line was empty.

Grandpa found my fish in the dust a ways back down my trail. My aunt took a photo of me with my 4½-pound lunker, and my catch was reported in the local paper.

It changed my life. I would pursue fishing from then on, eventually buying Buck Creek Marina on Bull Shoals Lake on the Missouri-Arkansas border, and working as a fishing guide for 25 years.

Since then, I've caught many fish larger, but none that thrilled me as much.

FRED RICHARDSON · PROTEM, MO

Saddle Up!

My son Richard loved his jumping horse. He was
18 months old when I took this photo in February 1959.

BILL YOUNG · ONEIDA, NY

CHAPTER 2

ALL IN THE FAMILY

These stories of cherished time with relatives and charming photos with siblings will encourage you to dust off your own photo albums.

MAY · 55

Proud Granddad

My great-uncle John Gross has his hands full with his grandchildren—my cousins Richard and Barbara—in Philadelphia, Pennsylvania, in 1948.

MIRYAM GROSS · MONSEY, NY

Grandma's Alpine Dream

Elegant midcentury dishware represents
single mom's hopes.

Sliding open the thick glass door of Grandma's buffet, I looked closely at her dishware, which she acquired in the early 1960s by saving grocery-store promotional stamps.

Dad, his wife, my three siblings and I were cleaning out Grandma's apartment after her death. She lived on the first floor of our Chicago three-flat with some or all of us since the 1980s. She and my parents bought the building together when I was 9 years old. When my siblings and I were young, Grandma helped our parents with babysitting. As she

aged, we helped her by bringing her groceries and checking on her daily.

My parents moved in and out of the upstairs rooms through divorces and remarriages. Tenants came and went. My sister and I lived on the third floor during our college years. Through it all, Grandma, Reba Mae Eskridge Springsteen, was a constant. She'd sit in her favorite armchair near the picture window, watching Chicago Cubs games and soap operas on her TV. We grandchildren visited with our dogs and cats and then our own children until the day she died.

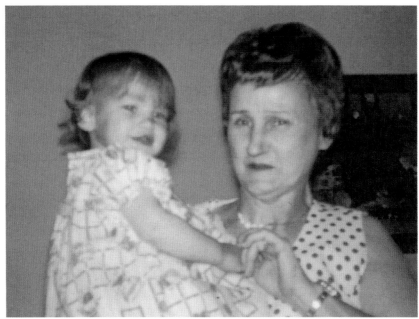

Stephanie grew to love her Grandma Reba Mae's Swiss-themed dish set.

*The pattern is called Swiss Chalet or Swiss Alpine—
ironic, as Grandma never skied a day in her life,
much less visited the Swiss Alps.*

Grandma had collected the dishes early in her marriage, before Grandpa walked out. After he left, she moved with her three sons back to the city, where she sometimes worked two jobs.

Throughout our childhood, my sister Rachel and I, influenced by our mother's taste, had never been fond of Grandma's dishes. We preferred the country style popular in the 1980s. But in the early 2000s my husband, a graphic designer, introduced me to midcentury modern style. About the same time, our neighbors, also designers, showed me their vintage Temporama dishes, and I was surprised by how similar they were to my grandma's. It gave me a new appreciation for her collection.

I researched Grandma's dishes and discovered they were made by the Stetson China Co. of Chicago and distributed by Mar-crest. The pattern is called Swiss Chalet or Swiss Alpine— ironic, as Grandma never skied a day in her life, much less visited the Swiss Alps.

It wasn't until many years after she died that I realized what the dishes must have meant to her. They symbolized not just her persistence in collecting all those grocery stamps but also an aspiration—a snapshot of how life was supposed to be when she married my grandpa and had three children. That dream was postponed when my grandfather left her, yet she kept the dishes and therefore kept the dream as she moved from place to place, raising her boys and working.

Today, I proudly display her dishes in the blond wood Ikea cabinets in our kitchen. They perfectly complement the simple Swedish aesthetic.

Every morning I lift the turquoise lid of the sugar bowl to sweeten my coffee and it reminds me of the times Grandma and I ate breakfast together. I use the dishes on holidays or whenever I need a little extra comfort. And every time I use them, I feel she is with me.

STEPHANIE SPRINGSTEEN · CHICAGO, IL

Potato Salad Days

Mom's cooking was a grilling experience.

My mother, Nancy, used to say that when your mother was really good at something, you didn't learn to do it. My grandmother was an accomplished seamstress, baker and cook. My mother was an adequate cook for our family of seven. We didn't starve; we had meat, potatoes and another vegetable at every meal—corn, green beans or peas. Out of a can. Hey, that was the pinnacle of healthy eating in the 1950s.

I was told that Mom could make amazing coffee. I liked the smell but couldn't tolerate the taste. It was the old-fashioned kind that percolated on the stove and brewed for what seemed like the whole day.

Baking was not Mom's forte, but on Saturday mornings, she was skilled at sending us to the bakery for fresh cake. I loved riding my blue Schwinn down the hills to buy a coffee cake.

Mom did learn to make the foods Dad, Kleff, loved—bacon and eggs, spareribs, sauerkraut and, especially, potato salad.

Potato salad was my mom's signature contribution to every summer party, although eating a mayonnaise-rich dish on a hot July day could be like playing with grenades.

Case in point: the time my uncle and aunt and their six kids picnicked at the lake with us. The menu included burgers on the grill, burnt to a crisp or slightly raw—take your pick!—lots of pop, s'mores and Mom's potato salad.

We spent hours at the lake. So did the salad.

Looking back, polishing off Mom's potato salad may have been the catalyst that finally inspired Dad to build us a second bathroom.

Which only proves that everything can have a silver lining if you think about it.

JEANNE ANDERSON · GENESEO, IL

Jeanne's mom, Nancy, above, had a special picnic dish.

Learning to tie shoelaces is a step forward in childhood, as it is for this pint-size New Yorker in 1948.

Close Ties

Dad's patience forges a tight knot.

The day I learned to tie my shoes still brings to mind cherished memories of my dad.

Not quite 6 in 1952, I was anxiously looking forward to beginning first grade. My mom recently finished making some new clothes and buying new shoes for me.

The shoes were black-and-white saddle oxfords, typical schoolgirl shoes back then. I thought they were very pretty and was certainly proud of them. But I fretted about what I would do if they became undone while I was at school, because I didn't know how to tie them.

Living on a small tobacco and crop farm in the foothills of North Carolina, and being something of a tomboy, I spent considerable time with my dad. I helped him—at least, I believed I was helping—with chores. I would do things like hand him the tools he needed when he was repairing something. Dad was a jack-of-all-trades when it came to fixing things and solving problems. Plus, his work shoes did up with laces. That, in my mind, made him the perfect person to teach me how to tie shoes.

He very slowly and patiently showed me the steps a few times, and then had me try to copy what he did. After several attempts, I got it!

I happily and proudly wore my new saddle oxfords to school. I could tie the laces so well that they hardly ever needed retying. Even now, whenever I tie a lace, ribbon or bow, I think of the wonderful times I spent with my father.

EVELYNN HEFNER · LENOIR, NC

DEAR OLD DAD

PILE UP!
I had just enough room for my kids Mindy Sue, 5, and David McKinley, 1½, on my lap in the late 1950s.
DAVID BUTTON
ROSWELL, NM

BE FRUITFUL AND MULTIPLY
After 13 boys in a row were born to student couples at Wartburg Seminary in Dubuque, Iowa, we signed them up for a "Men for the Ministry" conference in 1957. The new pastors would have graduated in 1983, but, unfortunately, none of the boys followed in their father's footsteps. I'm the fifth dad from the left.
EUGENE GAUERKE · WAUPACA, WI

THE JOY OF COOKING

My dad, George Fortier Sr., was an interior decorator by trade, but he loved to cook. He made chicken dinners for church volunteers, and his summer lobster bakes at Matunuck Beach were famous. Here, he's making our holiday meal in 1976.

CONSTANCE BOISVERT · WOONSOCKET, RI

Oh, Brother!

She hoped for something more girly.

When I was 7, Mom announced an exciting change was on the way—she was expecting another baby. With an older and younger brother already, I knew all I needed to know about boys—another one could only mean trouble—and so I intended that this sibling would be a sister.

I began to prepare for her arrival. I embroidered a baby jacket, following Mom's gentle suggestion to choose yellow, rather than pink. I also asked Santa for a doll carriage big enough for the real baby that would come soon after Christmas. When I prayed, I used all my authority to direct God to make sure Mom's baby was a girl. I could imagine nothing else.

One day in January, my parents left for the hospital while our grandparents waited at home with us kids. Soon, Dad returned to announce the arrival of my newest sibling. It's a moment I'll never forget: With a huge grin, Dad said, "It's a boy!"

Another brother? I was dumbstruck. Disbelieving. Mad! As the boys hooted, I held on to a glimmer of hope: Dad was pulling my leg. "I won't believe it until I see it!" I said.

Once home, Brother No. 3 continued to disappoint. Although little Jimmy looked cute in the jacket I'd made for him, it only fit him for two weeks. The doll carriage was another letdown, as he quickly outgrew it, too. Mom explained that most babies don't come into this world weighing 11 pounds, as my new brother did.

My wish for a sister was never granted, but I got used to carving a place for myself in a world of brothers. I played G.I. Joe, cowboys and Indians and chess with them, and served as substitute carrier on the boys' paper routes. But none of them could ever be persuaded to let me stay in their room—with its coveted bunk beds, and where all the action was—while one of them stayed in mine.

Baby Jimmy is the center of attention in 1958.

Years later, Jimmy and I shared a love of music and dedication to piano lessons. We sang along to records and memorized lyrics of musicals. When I was old enough to drive, he and I went to see *Oliver!* and *West Side Story*.

Friends of mine said I was really lucky because I didn't have an irritating sister borrowing my clothes. I knew I was really lucky because I had three brothers I learned to treasure.

LYNNE STADER · WESTFORD, MA

Bill cherishes the sailor suit his mom made so he could look like his adored big brother, David. In this photo taken in 1960 in Clinton, Iowa, Bill is 6 and David 18.

Little Sailor, Big Sailor

Imitation can be the highest form of love.

A gap of 12 years and three sisters are between my brother, David, and me. He was always at a different place in life. When I was in kindergarten he was graduating high school and heading off to the Navy.

For a little boy, this made for an unusual life experience growing up. Anything that belonged to my big brother was something I wanted to keep. The collection has included a phonograph, vinyl albums, a 35 mm camera, an electric road-race set, and several objects from David's time in the Navy.

When I was in elementary school, I never wanted to say goodbye when it was time for him to go. I would disappear into a closet or some other secluded spot until he had gone. In my mind this was easier than saying farewell when I really wished for him to stay.

I've had many wonderful times with my brother since then, but I still feel a loss from those younger days. Hence, my insistence to hold on to things even as life now requires some downsizing. One of my most prized items is the sailor suit that our dear mom, Anna, made for me when I was in kindergarten. Then, as now, I looked up to my big brother and desired nothing more than to be like him.

BILL BROWN · NORTH RICHLAND HILLS, TX

Pleasures of Childhood Revived

Reliving the delights of decorating in miniature.

Since she was a child growing up in the 1940s, my mother, Linda Hick Decker, adored her little tin dollhouse. Kids had few toys back then, so her dollhouse was a cherished treasure and source of exciting childhood memories. On Saturday mornings, while her mother cleaned, her father would take her to Laser's five-and-dime store in Bristol to add to her collection of dollhouse furniture. Years later, Emma Laser sold her store, which became Bob's Chalet Ski and Snow. Coincidentally, I worked at Bob's as a bookkeeper for 23 years. To think that Mother walked on that same floor as a child 50 years earlier, choosing her tiny trinkets!

Somehow, during the passage of time and the process of growing up, my mother lost her little tin dollhouse. As an adult, on a mission to find another one, she kept an eye on tag sales and antique shops. She finally did come across an exact replica and snatched it up. This prompted a new search. Instead of spending Saturday mornings with her dad at Laser's, my mother spent Saturday mornings with me, combing through yard sales as we hunted for dollhouse furniture.

We recently began redecorating the dollhouse, embellishing it with handmade curtains, dishes, battery-powered lights and other accessories, including a miniature portrait of her mother in one of the bedrooms. It has been an ongoing pleasure filled with endearing memories for both of us.

CYNTHIA DECKER SARACENO · BRISTOL, CT

Linda enjoys fixing up her tin dollhouse with daughter Cynthia. A portrait of Linda's mother adorns the little bedroom.

Everyone grows into helping with the household chores eventually.

Tapped to Assist

When it comes to a challenge, be careful what you reach for.

Our family lived on South Delmar Avenue in eastern Dayton, Ohio. One snowy winter Saturday, my little sister Pat and I came in from a tiring day of sledding to find our mother, Pauline, hard at work in the kitchen.

Delicious aromas of pork, sauerkraut and mashed potatoes filled the house. As usual, we had to wash our hands before eating.

Rather than run all the way upstairs to the bathroom, I tried, as I had many times before, to reach the faucet handles at the kitchen sink. Alas, as a short 8-year-old, I couldn't quite make it.

Mom smiled, put her hands on her hips and said, "I'll give you 50 cents if you can reach those handles."

Holy moly! 50 cents! I could hardly believe it. This was 1948 and my weekly allowance was 15 cents. If only I could find a way to reach those handles, I'd be rich.

After supper I retreated to my bedroom to work on the problem. Finally, it occurred to me: What if I stuffed newspaper into the toes of my shoes?

Ten minutes later, I walked into the kitchen.

"Hey, Mom," I said, "let me try those faucets one more time."

Standing on tiptoe in my newly stuffed Buster Browns, I was just able to reach the cold-water faucet to turn it on, then off. Mom raised her eyebrows and praised me.

"Yes, but what about the hot water?" she asked.

Bursting with excitement, I then turned the hot-water tap on and off. I looked at my mother in triumph.

"OK, here's your 50 cents," she said. "And from now on, you get to help with the dishes."

That was not the last time I was to be reminded that my mother was a lot smarter than I was.

JOHN STRANG · MONTROSE, CO

AT HOME WITH HOOVER

Consumer icon evolves along with households over the 20th century.

1939 »

Workhorse to Princess

The 1939 Model 305 sports a version of the molded plastic housing styled by industrial designer Henry Dreyfuss, which transformed the vacuum.

« 1964

Canister Types

By the mid-'60s, canisters are the cool cousins in vacs— Hoover's old standby, the upright, isn't even pictured here. The Constellation, center, is still popular. And on-board tools finally arrive—both the Slimline and Portable models have them.

The new Hoover Celebrity.
The most powerful home
vacuum cleaner you can buy.

With the most powerful motor and the biggest bag anyone has ever put in a home canister vacuum. The 3.7 peak-horsepower motor* and the 13-quart dirt bag keep Celebrity cleaning strong. Long after other vacuums have called it quits. Ask your Hoover dealer to show you all the new and exclusive Celebrity features, like the remote on-off switch, edge cleaning, and push-button suction controls.

See the brand-new Hoover Celebrity today at your Hoover dealer.

*1.3 VCMA HP
Average test results as reported by an independent testing lab.

Hoover Celebrity.
The most powerful home vacuum cleaner you can buy.

1974   **Circling Back**
The Celebrity replaces the Constellation in the 1970s. One version of Celebrity bounces around on exhaust as its ancestor did, but this one has wheels for more controlled travel through the home. On-board tools now live outside the housing for quick access.

SIBLING HARMONY

TWIRLER OBSERVERS

Little sisters Diane and Julie had to wait for Charlotte and Kay to use the batons first on our farm in Edinburg, Ohio, in 1958. Mom made their matching dresses.
ROGER GORDON · AKRON, OH

BRIGHT AND SUNSHINY FACES

Leaving Sunday school in 1959 or 1960 are my brother Dale, me, our friend and neighbor Warren Berg and my sister, Patsy. The church, Amicable Congregational in Tiverton, Rhode Island, is still there.

KATHY AGUIAR
WESTPORT, MA

OH, THE SAN FRANCISCO SIGHTS

My sister, Helen, was 13 and I was 15 when we visited the Fleishhacker Zoo and the Cliff House in 1947. After Mom took this picture of us, we went to Fisherman's Wharf for a dinner of Pacific crab.

J.D. LOGUE
PATTERSON, CA

This Girl Allowed

A kid sister takes on the boys at their own game.

Most of the kids in our neighborhood in 1955 were boys. Whether playing games or building forts, they always followed an unwritten rule: No girls allowed.

I was 7 and spunky—the youngest in our family, with a brother two years older and a sister five years older. With few options for playmates, I challenged that no-girls rule.

The boys decided as a group that if I could pass a series of tests, I could join them. I had to climb a tree, hop a fence, run like the wind and hit a home run.

The first two were easy. The third I had already mastered. After years of pestering my brother, Ron, I learned to run fast as a survival skill.

Hitting a home run would be my biggest challenge and possibly my undoing. When I passed the first three tests, all of the boys were worried that I might succeed and that they would have to let me play with them after all. So not one of them would teach me the art of slamming a homer.

BALLPLAYERS: D. CORSON/GETTY IMAGES

Ron was a good pitcher, and I knew he would show me no mercy. His first pitch flew right by me. Strike one.

Our next-door neighbor was a medic in the Navy and home on leave. He and his college-age sister became my allies.

After they practiced with me secretly for a week, I confidently confronted my future playmates. We gathered in our makeshift baseball field, and the fielders, all smirking at me, took their positions. First base was the fire hydrant, second was Mr. Gray's Oldsmobile and third was Tommy's mailbox. You had to tag each one for it to be official. I stood at home plate waiting to see who was selected to be the pitcher. My confidence slumped as my very own brother, Ron, took the mound.

Ron was a good pitcher, and I knew he would show me no mercy. His first pitch flew right by me. Strike one. My brother's face showed no expression. I looked over at my mentors, Sandra and Jake, who nodded their encouragement.

At this point, Ron started acting silly and hamming it up for his audience. Then he lobbed one over home plate. I smacked it with all the power a 7-year-old could muster.

The ball rocketed over their heads and I flew around the bases. I touched the fire hydrant, Mr. Gray's Oldsmobile and then Tommy's mailbox.

I was rounding for home and victory when the outfielder gunned the ball. I heard it hit my brother's glove. From there, it was a quick toss to the catcher and I would be out, my hopes of joining the boys' club dashed.

But my brother fumbled it. As I crossed the plate, I looked at him. Ron smiled and gave me a wink.

BECKY SNIFFEN · BELLINGHAM, WA

Ithaca Is the Answer

Nine kids get Ivy League education.

My mother, Tazu Asai, was a second-generation Japanese American. The lineage of the Asai family originated with a high-ranking nobleman connected to a Japanese emperor. In 1902, her father, Monroe, married Kame Toyoda. Monroe's parents disapproved of the marriage, so in 1903 the young couple boarded a Canadian steamer, SS *Athenian*, at Kobe to immigrate to the United States. Their firstborn died on the voyage.

Following unsuccessful attempts at rice farming and running small restaurants—one in Houston, Texas, and another in Galveston—Monroe learned to grow vegetables and started a profitable farming business. His nine children all helped on the farm.

Monroe wanted a good education for his children. In 1920, when my mother was 12, Monroe moved the family to Ithaca, New York, where Cornell University is located. He became a poultry and dairy farmer, and all of his children went to Cornell.

My mother graduated with a degree in agriculture in 1931. Just as her father had, she dreamed of sending me, her only child, to Cornell. She worked as a secretary for a professor for more than 30 years, making me eligible for free tuition. I fulfilled my mother's dream by graduating with a fine arts degree in 1968.

CARA LAROSE · CLEARWATER, FL

Tazu, at top right, poses with her parents and eight siblings.

Twin calves Salt and Pepper enjoy pets from Gregory, Tricia and David in 1974.

Back to the Land

City family puts down roots on 40 acres in the country.

——

We were city folk, born and raised in a suburb on the east side of Detroit. David and I married in 1958, then the family started growing: Chris, Gregory, David, Scott and—surprise!—Tricia.

In 1969, when Tricia was 4 weeks old, we moved 200 miles north to a 40-acre farm with a large house. Everybody called the area God's Country, and told us we were crazy for moving up there.

Day-to-day life was much different from what we were used to. We had well water, a septic tank, a wood-burning stove for heat and a propane stove for cooking.

Naturally, we had a garden, and I canned vegetables, as well as apples, pears and plums from trees that grew right in our yard. When it came time to tap the trees for maple syrup, I learned the hard way not to boil down the sap in the house. Oh, the humidity!

The kids watched deer, rabbits and raccoons— and avoided skunks after one sprayed our dog. They also loved to just sit in the woods and listen to the leaves.

The farmyard animals kept us busy too. We raised chickens and kept turkeys and geese. Some animals had to go after we learned their habits: The pigs rooted up the barn's basement walls and the goat jumped onto our car. Billie and Lucky were our Welsh ponies, and Salt and Pepper were the twin calves.

Life on the farm was a challenge, but the neighbors were wonderful, and we all loved it.

SANDY FAVOR · CADILLAC, MI

Great Ape Escape

Imaginations go wild at the zoo.

My daddy, Alex, scooped Betty Mae onto his shoulder and tugged Jenny along by the hand.

"The orangutan got loose!" he said.

I did my 8-year-old best to keep up with Daddy's long strides as we hurried through a wooded area at the Brookfield Zoo west of Chicago.

The car doors closed behind my sisters and me, and Daddy smiled and breathed a deep sigh of relief. "We made it! That orangutan won't be able to get us now."

As we drove away from the zoo, I thought about the huge ape from whom Daddy had kept us safe.

From behind a small wrought-iron fence, we had stared, fascinated by the orangutan behind the bars of his cage. A massive lump of long red-brown hair,

he had huge jowls and leathery hands at the end of long arms. He blinked his bright black eyes at each one of us, making us wonder what he was thinking.

We moved closer to Daddy as he said in a serious voice that expressed great respect, awe and a smidgen of fear, "That's the orangutan!"

A long time afterward, I looked back on that summer of 1938 when our father saved us from the orangutan that got loose. I remembered his happy, triumphant look after we sped through the woods and sat safely in the car, and it dawned on me that he was just having fun with us. What a gift to have a tall-tale-telling dad whose imagination brightened my world.

LAVERNE MILLER · TINLEY PARK, IL

Two of a Kind

George and I were a year apart, but our mom, Helen,
often dressed us alike. This was Memorial Day 1943.

LOUIS C. BARKOVICH · PAW PAW, MI

CHAPTER 3

·····························

TRUE LOVE

From first romantic encounters to wedded
bliss, get to know darling couples and
their heartwarming narratives.

Prince Charming

I lived two blocks from Al Meinen, but we went to separate schools.
After my friend stood him up, I started talking to the tall, handsome boy.
My family teased me about dating the dark-haired "Prince Albert." We
married in September 1952; seven months later, Al went into the Army.

JEANNINE MEINEN · BELLEVILLE, IL

Deliriously Happy

Honeymoon in a hospital suite.

With her wedding ceremony only five hours away in 1959, my mother, Diane, thought Oscar, her intended (and my future dad), was playing one of his pranks. The nuptials would be allowed to go on under one condition: Oscar could attend the ceremony, but then he had to check himself into Harris Hospital in Fort Worth, Texas.

Diane had heard the rumor that Oscar's cousins planned to somehow make her miss her honeymoon—revenge for the stunts Oscar had played on his relatives on their wedding nights through the years. But this turned out to be no prank. Oscar had been diagnosed with double pneumonia.

Diane paled; guests were coming and the church was ready. Oscar said, "We can still begin our future. It'll be something we can tell our grandchildren about."

The doctor gave Oscar antibiotics and steroids. With a flushed face and sweating through his wedding suit, Oscar waited as his beautiful and beaming bride walked down the aisle on her father's arm. Oscar and Diane exchanged vows, rings and kisses, ate some cake and were showered with rice. Then, tailed by scheming cousins, who suspected Oscar of deceit, the couple took the car straight to the hospital where Dr. Gibbs was waiting.

There, Oscar nearly fell into his hospital bed, relieved to have made it through the ceremony without fainting. The wedding photographer came with them to the room, and Mom leaned in toward Dad for a most unusual honeymoon picture, which was later featured in the *Fort Worth Star Telegram*—proof to his cousins he wasn't faking.

KATHY THOMAS · NORTH RICHLAND HILLS, TX

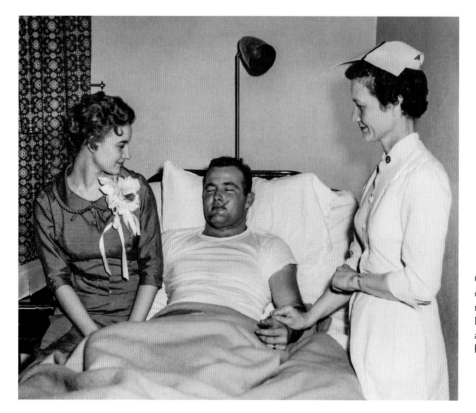

Ceremony over, Oscar rests with Diane and a nurse at his side.

Chuck first spotted Syd when she danced in a playhouse production.

Cyd & Chuck

He found his dance partner in the phone book.

Halfway through my two years in the Army, my job was operating the closed-circuit radio station at Fort Gordon, which is a few minutes southwest of Augusta, Georgia. At that time, Sydney Ann Shields was a high school senior in that city, although I didn't know her yet.

I was a stage-struck boy from south Georgia, and I went to see a Post Playhouse musical production called *Masquerade*. There I saw Syd and her dazzling dance skills for the first time.

The next day, I pulled out the Augusta phone book and called each Shields listed until I found her. Nervously, I explained to her that I was looking for a dance partner to learn some numbers for possible area bookings. Her response: "My mom and I would be happy for you to drop by our apartment, if you like." I liked!

I can only describe the ensuing months as magical, as Syd and I performed shows as Cyd & Chuck and taught dance classes. We fell in love.

My college training was in education administration. Even before my discharge from the Army, I applied for, then got, a job as an elementary school principal near the small town of Blythe, outside Augusta.

Syd and I were married on Aug. 21, 1955, and have five children who are thriving. But when I allow myself the luxury of recalling the past, I almost want to go back in time to those early delightful days together.

CHUCK BOWEN · MOULTRIE, GA

Love letters between Lance and Rory flew back and forth across the ocean.

1,000 Ways to Say I Love You

Two devoted correspondents get it right.

Separated by thousands of miles, my girlfriend, Rory, and I had to invent ways to say "I love you." We had no trouble at all expressing our feelings when we were together, but when I enlisted in the Air Force in July 1965, the only way to stay in touch was through writing letters.

I spent 30 of my 48 months in uniform overseas, so we wrote a lot of letters. Our first efforts were a little amateurish, but I was barely 18 years old when I left, and Rory was only 15.

My first permanent duty assignment was at Clark Air Base in the Philippines. Letters took an average of seven days to cross the Pacific, so when one of us asked a question, the answer was two weeks away.

I made it home for her high school graduation in June 1967, and then I was off to Travis Air Force Base, outside Fairfield, California.

Hundreds of miles apart, at least we were in the same state. Again, we wrote and wrote.

We got engaged while I was home on leave in July 1968, and then I served what felt like a very long year at Tan Son Nhut Air Base in Vietnam. By then we'd had lots of practice writing letters, but it was back to a two-week wait for an answer to a question. Rory added "P.S. - Be Careful and Be Mine" to every letter.

I wrote often to reassure her that I was OK. We wrote the last letters to one another early in July 1969. I arrived home safe, sound and discharged a week before Neil Armstrong walked on the moon.

All of our scribbling worked, since we recently celebrated our 50th wedding anniversary. And we still have those letters—all 1,076 of them!

LANCE EDMISTEN · MODESTO, CA

Drive-In Meetup

It took a year—and a lucky connection—to say hi.

Times were simpler when my good friend Herman Fields and I rode our bicycles 7 miles from our homes in Osawatomie to the swimming pool in Paola.

One day when I was 14, we arrived to find only one other person in the pool. I had never paid much attention to girls before, but I noticed this one. She was wearing a black swimsuit and had long black hair. Sitting at the top of the slide, she was the prettiest girl I'd ever seen.

I didn't have the courage to talk to her, but I did everything I could to get her to notice me. She didn't.

A year later, I was working at the local drive-in theater. I was friends with the projectionist, and after the show started, I went to his booth to talk with him. Who should walk past but the girl with the long black hair.

"I've got to meet that girl!" I said.

I couldn't believe it when my friend said, "My sister?"

That time I had the courage to catch up with her and start a conversation. Her name was Loretta.

Several weeks later, I got my driver's license, along with my first car. I immediately called Loretta and asked her out. Our first date was to the drive-in— her parents went, too, and parked right beside us.

Loretta and I continued to go out for the next seven years, although not without numerous breakups among the many dates. In January 1966, we got married.

Like anyone, we've had our ups and downs, but I still would not change a thing. I'm as much in love with Loretta now as I was the first time I saw her.

THOMAS CROZIER · OSAWATOMIE, KS

Loretta and Tom are ready for their honeymoon in 1966.

Box of Glam Essentials

On-a-whim bid fulfills an earlier fancy.

L eaving the Conestoga Auction Co. parking lot in rural Lancaster County, I shook my head at my own weakness. Why in the world had I left a bid on that item? With luck someone else would want it, because if I brought it home, Elaine, my wife of 57 years, would jam her hands on her hips and roll her eyes.

"Don't forget, we're downsizing," she'd reminded me that morning.

I had exercised admirable restraint browsing the supersize picnic tables mounded with Christmas decorations, dishes, prints, books, trays of costume jewelry and family scrapbooks.

But I stopped dead in my tracks when my eyes settled on the dresser set. The contents of the gold case stirred visions of a 1940s Barbara Stanwyck brushing her hair.

How I decided to leave an absentee bid of $75, I don't know. Going home, I breathed a prayer: *Lord, please tell someone to outbid me.*

"So, did you find any treasures?" It's what Elaine always asked when I returned from the auction.

"Nah, just the usual stuff."

A call to Conestoga the next morning confirmed my fears.

"You won one item," the clerk said. "It's a, uh, dresser set. Sir? Sir, are you there?"

"Yes," I finally managed to say. "I'll pick it up this afternoon."

Later, while Elaine hauled yet another box from the attic, I slipped down to my basement office and shoved the dresser set under the sofa.

Months passed and I had tucked the dresser set away in a dark recess of my memory. Of more concern was the box of letters Elaine had found from before our marriage. She'd snicker or laugh at what I'd written to her when she was living in New York, taking classes at the Grace Downs School and working part time at Bergdorf Goodman. I was far away, a lovelorn student at Thaddeus Stevens Technical College in Lancaster.

It was the day before Valentine's Day when Elaine handed me one of the letters. "You should read this. It's from my mother to you."

I had no memory of this letter my mother-in-law, Della, had written me in the weeks before

Christmas 1955. I read: "Hello Bob, The reason why I didn't write sooner is because I didn't know what she really would like. I wrote her a letter asking for a few suggestions and these are the ones she has mentioned: a dresser set…"

I stopped. Elaine wanted a dresser set for Christmas more than 60 years ago? My memory is not what it was, but I knew I hadn't bought her one. Remembering the item I'd shoved under the sofa, I thought, *Della made me bid on that set!*

For Valentine's Day, I gave Elaine a box of antique valentines for her collection (which will never fall to the downsizing ax). Then I said, "There's something else. It's a Valentine's Day gift from me and your mom."

Elaine opened the box, and her hands flew into the air with delight. "It's beautiful! I love it! Whatever possessed you?"

When I told her the story, Elaine's eyes glistened. "We're keeping this," she said. "And we're handing it down. With the letter."

ROBERT KOZAK · LANDISVILLE, PA

A vintage dresser set reminded Robert of Old Hollywood elegance in scenes such as the one at left with Jean Harlow in *Dinner at Eight* (1933).

Ride-Share Romance

Wherever she's going is on his way.

O n my first day of classes as a college sophomore in Stevens Point in the late 1950s, an instructor had all of us students introduce ourselves. I learned that one classmate had gone to a high school that was about a dozen miles from mine in Phillips.

After class, that girl was waiting for me by the door. She asked me whether I had a car and would be willing to give her rides home on the weekend. That's how I met Carole.

The next year, she transferred to another college and we wrote a few letters to stay in touch. In one, Carole told me she'd be home for Christmas. She explained that her brother-in-law was playing in a band for a party on New Year's Eve. Carole wanted to attend the party, which was in a town 40 miles away: Would I give her a ride?

I didn't have anything else to do, so I accepted her invitation. I picked her up at her country home, and we drove my sleek 1957 Chevy to the party, where we danced, drank soda and talked about college classes. At midnight, we sat at our table watching everyone else hugging and kissing.

It was a typical northern Wisconsin night—10 degrees below zero. After the party, we bundled up, and as we waited for the car to warm up, we leaned in close and kissed.

Wow! It felt as if all the snow had melted and spring had arrived early. We cruised the 40 miles home, floating on air.

Carole and I continued to date, then got married and raised seven children together. I did a stint with the Marines, and we both completed college and became teachers, although at one time our teaching positions were 250 miles apart. I later sold that '57 Chevy to pay for part of my graduate school.

LADDIE ZELLINGER · PHILLIPS, WI

Carole takes a seat on Laddie's '57 Chevy.

Pick of the Litter

Ingenious plan to ask frosh was all his—or was it hers?

———

During my junior year at McHenry High School in 1947, one of my classmates, Rita Bolger, planned a hayride. The early night ride on a hayrack would meander over gravel roads in the picturesque, hilly countryside of our community, which is about an hour northwest of Chicago.

Whom should I ask to the party? We boys were supposed to invite junior girls, but one of my friends had asked a sophomore. My great idea was that I'd be able to choose the best date from among the freshman girls—the pick of the litter, so to speak—since they were new to the dating game.

A girl named Doris Bauer often came to the back of study hall, where I usually sat, and attempted to talk to me. She was really quite stunning, and had a great personality; she often quietly asked me all kinds of questions. I didn't know how to ask her to the hayride, however: As a junior, I knew it would hurt my pride if a freshman said no. My sister Darlene was good friends with Doris, and I asked her whether she thought Doris would go with me.

As I hurried past the superintendent's office on my way to catch the train home after football practice, I spotted Doris sitting by the pay phone.

"What are you doing here?" I asked.

Doris gave me her best *Mona Lisa* smile. "Darlene said you wanted to ask me something."

I asked, and Doris was ready with a definite yes. "It will be my first date," she said. "I've already called and asked my mother."

We married in 1954, and had three fine boys—my great idea to pick a freshman turned out very well. Doris died in 2020, and I miss her very much. And I wonder, was my pick destiny or pure chance?

DUANE ANDREAS · MCHENRY, IL

Janice brought a heifer to the fair in Palco, where she spotted Keith in the parade.

Tall in the Saddle

Horseman is the center of attention.

Even though my grandparents Keith and Janice grew up only a few miles apart, the first time they saw each other was at a parade in Palco, Kansas, in 1953. Janice was just shy of 14 and Keith was 15.

Keith was in the parade, carrying an American flag and riding a horse that belonged to his buddy John. Spooked by the marching band, the horse shied and tried to walk backward. Janice saw the boy up on the horse and noticed his blue eyes and wavy hair.

After the parade, Keith asked Janice if she wanted a ride and she said yes.

The couple dated all through high school, were married in June 1957 and raised three kids, including their son Kelly, who adopted me when he married my mom. How lucky to have pictures of the day that all of this was set in motion!

Now I bring my husband and our two sons to visit the farm in Kansas, so I can reminisce about playing in the dirt, riding in the combine and running in the wheat fields after harvest—and so that my boys can make their own memories of my grandparents.

JEN MCDANIEL · GALLATIN, TN

METAL FOR THE MRS.

Presents to last a marriage—or longer.

Paul Revere's Legacy

Revere Copper and Brass Inc. devised the method of adhering copper to the base of stainless steel pots, and debuted Revere Ware at the 1939 Housewares Show in Chicago. In the early 1950s, the cookware enjoyed premium status and would have been a welcome gift for any home cook.

Aluminum for All

Founded in Pennsylvania in 1901, the Aluminum Cooking Utensil Co. promoted the then-expensive metal as the material of the modern home. Its handy Wear-Ever turkey roaster appeared in the mid-1930s. Many still do the job in thousands of kitchens at holiday time.

Continued from page 65

« 1947

Mastering Toast

Originally marketed to restaurants, the pop-up toaster hit home kitchens in the 1920s. This steel-and-Bakelite Toastmaster is similar to the first designs sold in 1926. Here, happy homemakers show off the new perks that make it easier to use and clean.

You can go more, read more, visit more, play more, care more, or just relax...in the hours you save with an automatic dishwasher.

United States Steel

h Gifts of Steel

"She's getting married!"

Remember when they said that about you? Remember the excitement and the plans you made . . . the thoughts of a new and wonderful life *together* . . . the feeling of fulfillment knowing that your most cherished dreams had at last come true!

Or, perhaps, for lucky you, that glorious time is still to come!

Part of the thrill when you live this dream-come-true comes from the good wishes of friends and family. And usually, they are expressed most tangibly in a shower for the bride.

But now there is a new idea in bridal showers . . . a Steel Shower! Shower the bride with gifts of steel! And there's something quite significant in the idea of a Steel Shower. For a steel gift is first of all enduring . . . as enduring as she wants her marriage to be. It's beautiful, too, and always useful.

Perhaps it will be a gift for her new kitchen . . . a gift of lustrous stainless steel or colorful enameled steel. It might be a lamp or hostess tables of smart, jet black steel for her living room. There are literally thousands of things to choose from . . . made by hundreds of reliable manufacturers. For steel is everywhere in the home and steel will serve her all the days of her married life.

So to carry your best wishes to the happy bride . . . at a shower, or at the wedding . . . make it a smart, lasting, useful gift . . . make it a gift of steel!

Only Steel can do so many jobs so well

Shower the bride with Gifts of Steel

United States Steel

AMERICAN BRIDGE . . . AMERICAN STEEL & WIRE and CYCLONE FENCE . . . COLUMBIA-GENEVA STEEL
CONSOLIDATED WESTERN STEEL . . . GERRARD STEEL STRAPPING . . . NATIONAL TUBE . . . OIL WELL SUPPLY
TENNESSEE COAL & IRON . . . UNITED STATES STEEL PRODUCTS . . . UNITED STATES STEEL SUPPLY
Divisions of UNITED STATES STEEL CORPORATION, PITTSBURGH
UNITED STATES STEEL HOMES, INC. • UNION SUPPLY COMPANY
UNITED STATES STEEL EXPORT COMPANY • UNIVERSAL ATLAS CEMENT COMPANY   5-07

« 1955   ≈ 1962

Woman of Steel

United States Steel Corp., based in Pittsburgh, Pennsylvania, did a series of ads through the 1950s and 1960s to promote the prospects of steel as a building block for living. The spots at left and above are aimed at women—the 1955 ad ran in *Ladies' Home Journal*, the 1962 ad ran in *Life*—and show an array of home appliances made with the durable alloy. These ads have the tough task of selling the product behind another product, which can be awkward and baffling. They do it by focusing on a lifestyle message—in this case, it's the claim that steel makes life better.

ROMANCE IS IN THE AIR

BAND BONDING

Danny and I were both in the high school band in Beaver Falls. Danny drove several of us to band camp in East Palestine, Ohio, in the summers, in his beloved 1939 Ford. This is Danny and me, and the Ford, in 1950, right after graduation.
NORMA DURHAM
BEAVER FALLS, PA

FOR THE LONG HAUL

With six people watching, my grandparents Ronald and Diane Bronner got married after a whirlwind romance. They recently celebrated their 60th wedding anniversary, showing that when you're meant to be together, you somehow just know it.
ETHAN BRONNER
COLORADO SPRINGS, CO

1952

SHORTS NOTICE

Emanuel Crisalli's sister-in-law Grace tried to set him up on a blind date with her neighbor Elsie in Van Nuys, California. Neither was interested—until one day, when Emanuel was helping his brother outside, he spotted Elsie across the street. She was mowing the lawn in yellow shorts. Emanuel told Grace to set up a date.

Elsie and Emanuel got married in 1952, had three children—David, Ann Marie (me) and Davette—and celebrated their 60th anniversary in 2012.

ANN MARIE EBERHART · GIG HARBOR, WA

1962

2012

State parks fit Barbara and Don's wedding budget in 1956.

Honeymoon Camping

No-frills wedding trip lays groundwork for marital bliss.

Don and I were both still in college at Taylor University in Upland, Indiana, when we got married in June 1956. We were preparing for careers as medical missionaries—I was enrolled in the nursing program at Methodist Hospital in Indianapolis, set to begin in August. Don planned to follow me the next year to attend the hospital's medical technology program. All that is to say we had very little money, and wanted to keep our wedding arrangements simple.

We borrowed a tent, air mattresses, camp stove and other basic equipment, and after the ceremony, we headed north to Michigan. We did buy a can opener and a paring knife, as well as food for the five days we would be camping.

We camped at several state parks: Bay City in eastern Michigan, Higgins Lake in the north-central part of the state and Ludington on Lake Michigan's western shore. It was early in the season, so we had quite a bit of privacy for swimming, hiking and learning to work as a team preparing simple meals and cleaning up afterward.

The camping trip set a pattern of teamwork that continued for the 57 years of our marriage.

BARBARA LOVE · WEST UNITY, OH

Rebels at the Ritz

Couple meets on the ballroom floor.

A s I write the story of my parents' courtship, it seems as though I can hear the Big Band music.

Irene and Edward, my parents, met at the Ritz Ballroom in Bridgeport in 1949. They'd each declined to go when their friends initially invited them.

Irene, who was from small-town Milford, turned down her friends by saying Bridgeport wasn't somewhere that she usually went. Edward cringed at the idea of the dance hall: "I don't hang out in Bridgeport because I'm a New Haven boy," he told his friends.

At the ballroom, Edward spotted Irene, who was wearing bright red lipstick. He went across the dance floor, introduced himself and asked how old she was.

"19," she said

"Oh, only a teenager."

She was taken aback. With a smirk, he told her he was 21.

Despite this inauspicious beginning, the two hit it off. She wrote her telephone number inside a matchbook using Edward's back as a writing surface. Talking recently about their meeting, Mom pointed at Dad and said, "And I let this stranger drive me home."

Dad still has the gold watch Mom bought him that year; they got engaged before Dad left for two years of military service in Germany. They were married on Thanksgiving Day in 1952, and honeymooned in Washington, D.C.

Mom says, "He was a wise guy when I met him and he's still a wise guy today." I simply can't imagine either of them being married to anyone else.

ELLEN PAIVA · WALLINGFORD, CT

"He was a wise guy when I met him and he's still a wise guy today," says Irene.

Love Charm

Jeep necklace came with a promise.

M y mother, Gilberte, was born in 1927 in Saint-Denis, a suburb of Paris, France. Her father, Gabriel Farge, was a French officer in the First World War. Gilberte was a teenager during World War II, and lived through four years of Nazi occupation. She will always remember June 6, 1944, D-Day.

"My father came running into our home, shouting that the Americans were landing in Normandy."

She recalls that the people of the city were crying, laughing and dancing in the streets. She even remembers someone raising an American flag at the courthouse. After four years of German occupation and war, "It was like being born again."

My father, John Crowell, was part of the Normandy invasion, and was among the Americans who entered Paris after the city's liberation in August 1944. John, from Miston, Tennessee, met Gilberte at a dance and they fell in love. But the war wasn't over, and John had to return to the fight.

John served with the 752nd Engineering Company, and was part of the famous Red Ball Express that operated in the fall of 1944 to deliver gasoline, ammunition and supplies to the front.

Before he left to face the German army at the Battle of the Bulge in the winter of 1944-45, he gave Gilberte a necklace with a charm of an American soldier driving a jeep.

"I'll be back to marry you," he promised.

When the war finally ended, John returned to Paris. On July 4, 1945, Gilberte and her American GI were married at the courthouse in Saint-Denis.

In March 1946, Gilberte boarded the SS *Vulcania* in Le Havre to join John in the U.S. He met her in New York, and they flew to Muskegon, Michigan, where John's family had made their home. They raised four children there: Me (Jack), Jim, David and Dolly.

JACK CROWELL · MUSKEGON, MI

French-American alliance: Gilberte and John got married on July 4, 1945.

Carol followed George to his assignment in Greece in 1956.

Two Years in Greece

Family stays on shore while Coastie's at sea.

Carol and I married in 1955 while I was serving a tour of duty in the Coast Guard. In August 1956, our daughter Susan was born, and five days later I received orders to go overseas to Rhodes, Greece. Carol and our new daughter would be able to come to Greece, too, but Susan had to be at least 6 weeks old before the military would transport her.

I left without my family, departing New York on the troop transport the USS *Patch*. In Rhodes, I was stationed aboard the U.S. Coast Guard Cutter *Courier*, the radio ship for the Voice of America.

Carol was 19 that October, when she and Susan headed for Norfolk, Virginia; from there, the Navy flew them to Greece. She had little travel experience, and had never flown before. The trip took several days, and included stops in Bermuda and the Azores Islands.

I didn't know when Carol and Susan would arrive, so I was surprised when they called me on the ship. I was off duty, so I came ashore to spend the night with them and the next day we started hunting for apartments for Carol. She almost cried when she saw the tiny kitchens with their stone sinks and single gas burners.

Carol hired a local girl to help with the housework and the baby. The girl didn't speak English, and Carol was determined to practice her Greek with her.

Most of the time, the only way Carol and I could communicate was by mail, which we sent and received once a week.

My tour of duty finished in 1958. Carol and I were married for 62 years, and I thank God for the years we had together.

GEORGE CASSELL · KNAPP, WI

Telegraph operators Mary and John met while working at the same Manhattan company in the early 1920s.

Interoffice Telegram

Dots and dashes spell out romance.

A fter high school, my mother, Mary Shine of Queens, New York, took a course at Brooklyn Telegraph School to learn to operate a telegraph key to send and receive Morse code. In 1918, she went to work at the Postal Telegraph-Cable Co. in Manhattan. Telegraph operators had to supply their own equipment, so Mary bought a semi-automatic, or bug, telegraph key, which has stayed in our family.

At her workplace, Mary met another telegrapher, John Schwenk. He was self-taught, and had served as a telegraph specialist for the Army during World War I. After being discharged, he worked as an operator for the New York Central Railroad Co. He rented a telegraph key so that he could moonlight at the Postal Telegraph-Cable Co. There, he noticed the pretty red-haired telegrapher named Mary.

He was too shy to ask her out himself, so he persuaded his friend to see if Mary was interested in dating him.

"Let him speak for himself," Mary said. So John asked his question via telegraph and Mary sent back her answer: Yes.

Mary and John married two years later. She became the first telegrapher at McGraw Hill Publishing Co., and worked until their first child, Virginia, was born two years later.

EILEEN SCHWENK · KINGSTON, NY

Stylish Sightseers

Bill and I took in the beautiful views at Monterey during
a trip early in 1972. It's hard to believe that was 50 years ago.

BARB GILBERT · NAPA, CA

CHAPTER 4

FADS, FASHION, FUN

Remember the popularity of sofa beds,
dressing up to travel and playing pinball at
the arcade? Browse these pages and enjoy!

Stole in Time

Here I am glowing in a sateen gown and rabbit-fur stole before
my senior prom in 1965. Bill was my first steady boyfriend.

JUDI CARROLL · ESCONDIDO, CA

Formica forms a continuous surface in a 1950s bath.

Counter Culture

Formica is witness to a century of solid lifestyle choices.

First registered as a trademark in 1922, Formica now forms a significant part of the backdrop of our memories: struggling with homework on a fire-engine red kitchen table; angling for mirror space over a star-patterned counter in school restrooms.

"We're in an elevator in a trade center; you're leaning on our countertop," says Renee Hytry Derrington, design lead for Formica brand. "We're everywhere in your life."

Beginning in the late 1940s, Formica's cigarette-proof, seemingly wear-proof surface material became a design tool of modern living. Easy to clean and available in an array of colors and patterns, it suited everything from ocean liners to suburban bathrooms.

In recent years, the brand has seen new life as sculpture and in many other artistic applications—and in houses again as well. Designers and DIY enthusiasts alike are now embracing Formica at the dawn of its second century.

KATIE DOHMAN

1913

Daniel O'Connor and Herbert Faber discover that high-pressure plastic resins can be used to make electrical parts. Because the material replaces the mineral mica, the electrical engineers call the business Formica Products Co.

···················

1920s

Long before it's material for countertops, Formica is in American homes in a different form: The company's insulated boards make ideal bases for hobbyist radio sets.

···················

1930s

In 1931, chemist Jack Cochrane, the company's head of research, adds layers of aluminum foil under the top color, creating an effectively cigarette-proof laminate. This material is soon popular for night clubs and other public spaces. In the mid-1930s, the interior spaces in the RMS *Queen Mary* feature a pearlescent gray laminate that holds up to the rigors of luxury travel and the ocean liner's use as a troop ship during World War II.

···················

1940s

Formica switches to war-effort production in 1941. It makes bomb tubes, airplane propellers and 88 components for P-51 Mustang fighter planes.

By 1948, the postwar housing boom underway, the company focuses on decorative laminates. Formica designs are featured in Cincinnati's Terrace Plaza Hotel and the Skytop Lounge for Milwaukee Road's Olympian Hiawatha train.

···················

Skylark then

Boomerang now

1950s

In 1950, industrial designer Brooks Stevens creates the iconic Skylark pattern, later renamed Boomerang. Along with Raymond Loewy, who devises Formica's Sunrise design, Stevens is "part of the pattern language about optimism" that defined 1950s style, says Renee Hytry Derrington of Formica Corp.
In 1953, new production techniques allow for more bends and curves. The "vanitory," a combo vanity and lavatory sink, shows up in houses (left). "Because it was continuous, no water could get in," Hytry Derrington says. "It wasn't

industry standard then, but the midcentury modern movement was rethinking everything."

···················

1964

Formica is among several manufacturers exhibiting at the New York World's Fair, now regarded as a cultural high point of the modern age.

···················

1980s

ColorCore, a surface with a solid color and no brown edge, debuts in 1982. Architect Frank Gehry uses chips of it for a lamp sculpture at a design exhibition. On its 75th anniversary in 1988, Formica reissues the Boomerang pattern.

Brooks Stevens used Formica in the Skytop car he styled in the '40s for the Olympian Hiawatha.

And Babies Make Seven

It's any pullout port in a storm for this Navy family.

When I was 15 months old—in 1955—my twin siblings were born. We were now a family of seven living in Navy housing at China Lake in California, about 150 miles north of Los Angeles.

The area had very few single-family houses at the time. Like almost everyone else in China Lake, we lived in a duplex. Our portion had three bedrooms, a full and a half bath, and the other usual rooms (kitchen, living room and dining room). Space was tight, especially with three babies in the house.

My brother was 7 and my sister almost 10 when I was born. Each of them had a bedroom. Mom and Dad moved out of the master bedroom and installed three cribs for the twins and me. That left Mom and Dad with no bedroom to sleep in.

The solution? Two hide-a-bed sofas, which they had delivered from San Bernardino. My parents slept in the living room until I was 7. At that point, they bought 5 acres and began building our new home—we called it the ranch. We moved there in 1961. No more cramped space. And Mom and Dad finally had their own bedroom back.

In 1963, our family gained another sister. You can draw your own conclusions!

MARGARET A. CLARK · WALLA WALLA, WA

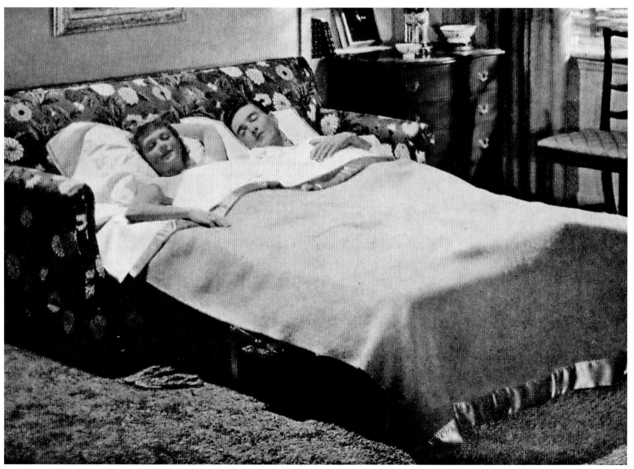

Sleeping in a 1950s sofa bed seems like a real dream for this couple.

Unfolding History

Hidden beds as a space-saving solution for apartments took hold in the late 1800s.

MARY-LIZ SHAW

A GOODE CABINET

In 1885, Sarah Elisabeth Goode of Chicago received a patent for a folding cabinet bed. Designed to

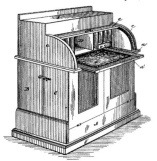

S. E. GOODE.
CABINET BED.
Patented July 14, 1885.

make maximum use of space, the piece was ideal for people living in large urban centers, where rooms in small apartments had to serve several purposes. Interlocking sections folded out into a single bed. Closed, it was a desk, with nooks for papers and supplies. Goode was one of the first African American women to receive a patent. According to *BlackPast.org*, little is known of Goode's life, except that both her father and her husband were carpenters, and it may have been through them that she gained her expertise in cabinetmaking.

....

MURPHY'S DILEMMA

The story goes that William L. Murphy devised his fold-up wall bed in the late 1890s while living in a one-room flat in San Francisco. He was courting an opera singer, and the era's strict etiquette prohibited a lady from visiting a man's bedroom. Our hero's workaround was to hide his bed behind a door. *Voila*—all upright parlor, no unseemly boudoir.

In fact, Murphy had tinkered with his invention for some time. And though his system employed ingenious mechanics (below), the concept of hiding a bed in plain sight wasn't entirely novel. Thomas Jefferson, for instance, had an affection for recessed alcove beds, and built one at Monticello in the 1790s.

Murphy patented his design, called the Disappearing Bed, in 1911. By 1925, he relocated the Murphy Wall Bed Co. to New York, where his design still enjoys legendary status.

....

CASTRO CONVERTIBLES

Now regarded as the father of the modern sofa bed, Bernard Castro founded his company in 1931 in New York with $400 he'd saved as an upholsterer. Beds that folded into seaters—called davenports (left)—existed then, but they weren't attractive or comfortable in either position. Castro's genius was in crafting foldouts that were beautiful and functional.

He was an early adopter of television advertising. Beginning in the late 1940s, his daughter Bernadette appeared in commercials opening a Castro couch, with the tagline "so easy, even a child can do it."

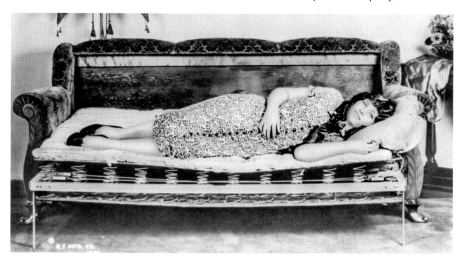

For Chris, taller than average, the couch had a steep learning curve when it came to sleeping in comfort.

Flat-Out Fun

The New Yorker answers need with stylish flair.

My wife, Peggy, and I started dating near the end of the school year at Brigham Young University in 1970. When the summer began, she went back home to work, while I stayed to work at the campus radio station. Our dates meant a round trip of 80 miles.

One Saturday night, we had tickets to a Glen Campbell concert, and we knew it would end late. Peggy's parents graciously invited me to stay over after the concert and then go with the family to church the next day. My assigned sleeping spot was in the family room downstairs on an orange Naugahyde couch in a style called the New Yorker.

Bright orange was a common decor tone at the time, but the shape of the couch was new to me. The backrest lifted off to increase the sleeping area. The seat cushion curled up at each end. It would make a convenient built-in pillow for most people, but I'm 6 feet 4 inches tall. Both my head and feet were elevated if I stretched out.

Over the summer, I slept on the New Yorker a few times, and I learned the best way to curl up to avoid its shortcomings. I grew rather fond of it.

Peggy and I married the following spring. Since the wedding ceremony was in the morning, I slept on the New Yorker the night before, eliminating any danger of sleeping in or getting stuck in traffic.

When Peggy's parents were redecorating, they offered us the New Yorker for our basement family room. Our children loved sitting on it to watch TV, and the slick finish was ideal for launching Hot Wheels off the sloped ends. Later, it migrated from our basement to Peggy's brother Mark's place.

Our daughter Kimberly loved the color orange, and Mark promised her the couch when she got her own house.

Naugahyde enjoyed a great reputation for durability, but after 40 years of family fun, the New Yorker was showing its age. The seat had a couple of small holes and stains, and the stitching was loose in spots. Even so, Kim proudly put it in her new living room.

One day, searching for fabric for a different project, Kim and Peggy found some orange Naugahyde that matched Kim's couch. After a complete restoration, the New Yorker is as unique looking as ever, and now is ready for the next generation to enjoy.

CHRIS BLACK · WEST JORDAN, UT

HAVE A SEAT (OR A BED)

Multifunctional furniture has been around for a while—is there some in your home?

Classic Lounger

Furniture pioneer Morris Futorian created the affordable Stratolounger recliner in 1952. It is based on the higher-end BarcaLounger design.

« 1973

Hiding in Plain Sight

Mattress maker Simmons produced its first sofa bed in the 1930s. This ad shows a stylish 1973 version.

Life in Pictures, in an Instant

50 years ago, Polaroid's new camera changed our view.

W ith a scientist's curiosity, Edwin H. Land, founder and CEO of Polaroid Corp., sought solutions to everyday problems. A Harvard dropout, he held 535 U.S. patents. His initial quest—to reduce nighttime glare from car headlights—resulted in his synthetic polarizer, which was patented in 1933.

But it was in 1943, when his impatient 3-year-old daughter demanded to see vacation snapshots "right now," that Land conceived of his most transformative product. Within an hour, Land had worked out the problem. Four years later, the Polaroid Land Camera Model 95 (far right), the first camera that could produce a developed print without sending the film out for processing, went on sale at a Boston department store.

The process wasn't instantaneous and it was messy. You clicked the shutter, cranked out a paper sandwich flooded with chemicals—nicknamed "the goo" at Polaroid—then waited about 60 seconds to peel off the top layer (while avoiding the icky goo) to see your print. Those first 95s produced only sepia-toned images, and picture quality couldn't compare to traditional film. But on-the-spot snapshots were irresistible. The cameras sold out in a day.

Land's dream reached its zenith in 1972 with the compact SX-70 camera, which spat out color prints without the user having to do anything but shoot and wait a bit.

Polaroid tapped a fundamental human urge for instant gratification that would propel consumer spending and inspire such world-changing inventions as the smartphone for years to come.

LINDA KAST

The SX-70 camera provided color prints to users after pointing and shooting and waiting briefly.

ONLY THESE TULIPS

To introduce the SX-70 at Polaroid's 1972 annual meeting, Land asked his head of international communications to order 10,000 Kees Nelis tulips, left, which have deep red and yellow blooms. Eelco Wolf later told *Smithsonian* magazine he had to fly them in from the Netherlands. Why that variety? With the SX-70's film still being perfected in the spring of '72, only reds and yellows showed true at that point.

. . . .

MAGIC BOX

Dubbed "Aladdin" to shield the project from competitors, the SX-70 was in the works for about 10 years. Its complex mechanics were housed in an elegant foldable casing of leather and brushed chrome over plastic. The design was overseen by Henry Dreyfuss, who also created designs for the Honeywell thermostat and the Hoover vacuum.

. . . .

QUITE THE SYSTEM

Achieving the simplicity of one-step photography in the SX-70 involved hundreds of advanced individual processes, according to Land. Among these was the dedicated film packet, which held enough for 10 exposures, plus the battery, relieving users of the worry their camera would run out of juice. In a promotional film about the SX-70, designers Charles and Ray Eames dubbed its workings "a system of novelties."

SHOW ME THE MONEY

The SX-70 retailed for $180 (more than $1,100 today) and suffered from early glitches, hurting sales. Polaroid had a larger profit on later, less stylish models.

. . . .

ARTISTS' DARLING

Artists as varied as Andy Warhol, above, Ansel Adams and Walker Evans embraced the instant imagery of the SX-70. Its nearly square 3⅛-by-3 1/16-inch prints allowed for unique compositions, such as David Hockney's portrait of two girls made up of 63 images arranged in a 9-by-7 grid.

POLAROID SNAPSHOT

The company began by setting trends, but then trailed in the shift to digital images.

1937: Edwin Land calls his company Polaroid Corp. after the trade name for polarizing film.

. . . .

1963: The Polacolor film pack debuts.

. . . .

1972: The SX-70, the first instant single-lens reflex camera, debuts shortly before Christmas.

. . . .

1981: Land resigns; Polaroid writes off $89 million after the ill-fated pursuit of Polavision, an instant movie system.

. . . .

2001: Ten years after Land's death, Polaroid seeks bankruptcy protection.

. . . .

2008: Polaroid stops making instant film.

TULIPS: REDA&CO/GETTY IMAGES; WARHOL: BROWNIE HARRIS/GETTY IMAGES
MODEL 95: THE KODAK COLLECTION AT THE NATIONAL MEDIA MUSEUM, BRAFFORD

An American Hero·

On the battlegrounds of Anzio, Iwo Jima, Seoul and Saigon; aboard ships crossing the oceans of the world; in planes and on land from coast to coast of the United States, the Zippo windproof lighter has earned the reputation as an American hero. Dependability and a famous life-time guarantee are only two of the qualities Zippo owners boast about. Our files are filled with stories of military men, law officers, pilots, outdoorsmen and ordinary people who owe their lives and safety to the durable, dependable, indestructible Zippo windproof lighter...an American hero.

Zippo

Zippo Manufacturing Co., founded in 1932 by George G. Blaisdell, has produced more than 500 million lighters.

Daniel bought this commemorative Slim lighter in the 1970s.

Rare Keepsake of a Special Time

Army engineer opts for an engraved piece of history.

W hile serving with the Army Corps of Engineers from 1975 to 1978, I traveled to many interesting places. But no experience compares to the six months I spent at Enewetak Atoll in the Marshall Islands.

There were 250 of us with the 84th Engineer Battalion, stationed out of Schofield Barracks in Oahu, Hawaii. We were tasked with clearing the island of Lojwa of its tropical sumac and turning it into a small city.

The United States had carried out considerable arms testing in the Marshall Islands in the 1950s. We were to clean up the area in order to return the territory to its people. We worked in 100-degree heat building thatched huts to live in. Then we

built a power plant, saltwater purification plant, multipurpose dining hall and helicopter pad.

Even at 19 years old, I realized this was a unique opportunity. I decided to mark the experience with a special-edition Zippo lighter that could only be purchased on the island during that time.

I put the old full-size Zippo I had used for years in my footlocker and bought a new Zippo Slim lighter engraved with the insignia of the Defense Nuclear Agency.

The lighter has stood the test of time and still works after 45 years. It never fails to bring back fond memories of my time in the Pacific.

DANIEL HOLDEN · AUBURN, NY

Duane's third Zippo marks a unique point in the Cold War.

Every Zippo Tells a Story

Three lighters define different stages in this sailor's life.

D uring my time as a smoker, three Zippo lighters found a spot in my pocket.

Zippo No. 1 came to me in 1967. It was bittersweet because it belonged to my grandfather, who had died from the effects of smoking. Whenever I used my grandfather's lighter, it reminded me of him, and it also reminded me that smoking was not a habit I should continue for long. My grandfather worked in oil-and-gas drilling; his lighter was engraved with a drilling rig. Sadly, my grandfather's lighter was stolen during my stint in the Navy.

I bought Zippo No. 2 in 1969 in the ship store of the USS *Forrest Royal*, which had been a destroyer in World War II. It had the likeness of the ship engraved on it. That lighter served me well as we deployed to the Indian Ocean and Caribbean Sea. But I lost it somehow and never found it.

Zippo No. 3 is perhaps the most interesting of all. It came to me because of the Cold War.

I mentioned that the *Forrest Royal* had been a vintage destroyer—as it and ships like it neared the end of their serviceability to the U.S. military, our government gave them to our allies to strengthen their navies against possible threats from the Soviets.

The *Forrest Royal* was to be given to the Turkish government. Early in 1971, sailors from the Turkish navy came aboard to train with us. Most of the American crew was reassigned. But 25 of us stayed on with the Turks to continue their training. We traveled with them to the naval yard at Philadelphia, where the ship was overhauled before going to Turkey.

A Turkish naval officer gave me the lighter as a token of gratitude and friendship. The Zippo features an engraving of the ship and her Turkish name, TCG *Adatepe*.

Though it is now more than 50 years old, the lighter still looks like new. I quit smoking shortly after I had received it, but it's certainly a cherished possession.

DUANE CLINE · HARTFORD, WI

Got a Light?

Smooth-edged, easy to hold and with a distinctive click, the Zippo quickly found a place in popular culture.

COUNTRY CLUB ORIGIN

At a golf course, George Blaisdell saw a friend struggle with an Austrian lighter. Its special chimney protected the flame in the wind, but the device took two hands to work, and it had a flimsy metal casing. Blaisdell, who grew up working in his family's machine shop, decided to make his own. He kept the chimney and restyled everything else.

....

WHY ZIPPO?

Blaisdell liked the word "zipper." He tried a few variations until he settled on Zippo. His first models cost $1.95, which would be about $38 today.

....

ENGRAVING WORK

In the mid-1930s, Kendall Refining Co. ordered 500 lighters embossed with its logo. Custom engraving quickly became key to Zippo's business model and status. Original Kendalls are collectibles.

....

WARTIME BOOST

Zippo shifted to the war effort in 1941, making a steel-cased lighter covered in a matte black "crackle" finish for U.S. troops (replica

seen here). Zippo lighters became indispensable. Famous war correspondent Ernie Pyle said a Zippo was "the most coveted item on the battlefield."

....

HOT CAMEOS

Zippo lighters have appeared in more than 2,000 movies and hundreds of small-screen productions. One of the more memorable bits occurs in *Die Hard* (1988) when Bruce Willis uses his

lighter to navigate an air duct (above).

....

ZIPPOS OF FAME

Celebrities from John Wayne to Matthew McConaughey have used or given Zippos as gifts. Eric Clapton's constant clicking of a Zippo wound up on "It's Probably Me," his 1992 recording with Sting. But few can beat Frank Sinatra for Zippo love—he was buried with one.

In the 1930s, Nestlé mixed coffee with sweetened milk before drying it to preserve taste and extend shelf life.

Instant Gratification

"Just add water" is the slogan of the dried-food era.

When Lipton introduced Cup-a-Soup 50 years ago, the trend for powdered and dried food that had been building for years took a new turn. The company already had a winner with its dried onion soup mix, introduced 20 years earlier. West Coast cooks elevated it to food legend by making it the key ingredient of California dip.

By 1972, cultural shifts contributed to the success of Cup-a-Soup and convenience food in general. In more than one-third of American households, both parents worked full time. Single-serve soups, among other child-friendly mixes, meant latchkey kids could help themselves to a snack after school.

Other trends helped, especially the letting go of strict proprieties about when food should be consumed—breakfast at 8, lunch at noon, dinner at 6. Now you could eat when you were hungry. And a hot meal didn't have to take hours—only as long as it took water to boil.

As Japanese entrepreneur Momofuku Ando, who introduced his Cup Noodles to Americans in 1973, observed, "I'm not selling instant noodles. I'm offering customers time."

MARY-LIZ SHAW

1909

Swiss chemist and pharmacist Albert Wander alters a malt extract his father, Georg, developed to combat malnutrition. He adds more palatable ingredients, including sugar, to create a hot drink, Ovomaltine, popular on ski slopes in Switzerland. In 1909, Wander introduces the beverage in the U.K. under the name Ovaltine.

....

1938

After years of trial and error, Nestlé brings a water-soluble coffee drink, Nescafé, to its Swiss consumers. Research began after the stock market crash of 1929, when the French and Italian Bank of South America was stuck with a surplus of Brazilian coffee after the price collapsed. Could Nestlé, the bank wanted to know, do something with all this coffee? Chemist Max Morgenthaler found that grounds mixed with high levels of carbohydrates preserved coffee aroma and taste. High pressure and temperature gave the mixture a longer shelf life.

....

1948

Nestlé Quik, an instant chocolate powder soluble in milk, debuts in the U.S.

Instant ramen noodles were an instant hit around the world.

1957

General Foods comes up with Tang, a sugary orange drink mix. In the early 1960s, the space program underway, NASA contracts with General Foods to buy the powder in bulk. So begins an association that Tang marketers will capitalize on for years. Tang was among several dried foods that accompanied John Glenn on his space flight in 1962, and it went with astronauts on the Gemini and Apollo missions.

....

1958

Japan's Momofuku Ando invents instant ramen—noodles ready to eat in two minutes by adding hot water. He opts for chicken flavor to entice his son Koki, who didn't like chicken, to try it. His choice proves to have global appeal. "There is not a single culture, religion or country that forbids the eating of chicken," Ando wrote in his 2002 autobiography.

1964

Carnation Instant Breakfast debuts. Ads claim that when mixed with milk, the drinkable meal has as much nutrition as a conventional breakfast of two eggs, two strips of bacon and two slices of buttered toast.

....

2013

Buzz Aldrin, Apollo 11 astronaut and the second man on the moon, tells Spike TV that he doesn't think Tang is very good. More than 2,200 respondents (29%) to a National Public Radio poll strongly disagree.

Tang advertising played up the drink mix's association with NASA. This ad from 1966 refers to the Gemini missions that began the year before.

Turfgrass

A perfectly green carpet of a lawn was important.

Along with the identical houses sprouting up in suburbs all across postwar America came matching plots of manicured nature. Lawns extended the indoors to the outdoors, providing recreational space for growing families. A weed-free swath of turf implied pride of ownership and marked a model citizen. Companies responded with new technology, such as lightweight aluminum push mowers and traveling sprinklers, for the army of amateur landscapers. *Saturday Evening Post* explored the cultural trend in an article titled "The Grass Craze" in 1962, the same year Merriam-Webster gave the compound word an entry.

NATALIE WYSONG

A powerful symbol of the American dream, the lawn around this suburban house serves as an outdoor living room for a couple in 1960.

Millions of women asked their hairdressers to re-create Farrah Fawcett's blow-dried style.

BLOW-DRIED

THE SEXUAL REVOLUTION OF THE 1960S AND '70S reshaped hairstyles, leading to longer, fuller coifs for both women and men. The carefree look of figure skater Dorothy Hamill's popular wedge cut and the natural, feathery layers famously worn by actress Farrah Fawcett were in fact high maintenance, requiring extensive blow-drying (and gobs of styling product). Merriam-Webster gave blow-dried an entry in 1977, the year after Hamill's Olympic championship and Fawcett's single season on TV's *Charlie's Angels*.

NATALIE WYSONG

WHO STARTED IT?

Hairstylist José Eber takes credit for inventing Fawcett's famous do, claiming he first wore the style himself.

HOW FASHIONABLE!

PRETTY IN PINK

These are my daughters Vicki and Kay in their new Easter outfits in 1958. Vicki pets Mopsy as Kay holds her pet rooster, which was a gift the previous Easter. Vicki's sparkle-framed sunglasses are a child's version of a popular fashion trend in women's glasses in the '50s.

AILEEN SHERRILL
CRAB ORCHARD, TN

COOL VIEW

My wife Louise "Lou" Crawford relaxes at Sliding Rock, North Carolina, in 1955, while on a first-anniversary vacation with me, from our Minnesota home. She's wearing a colorful skirt, short socks and flat shoes for day travel.

BOB CRAWFORD • APPLE VALLEY, MN

PROM AND PROPER

I'm beaming with delight at Tom Neppel's high school senior prom in 1972. I was a junior. He was this amazing jock. I was totally in love with him—in that teenage way. My parents insisted that my dress be prim and proper.

PHYLLIS GEBHARDT • SANFORD, FL

TRAIN TRAVEL

Even travel outerwear was crisp and stylish, as my mother Pauline Thompson shows in a picture taken sometime around the late '50s. She wears a smart red coat and matching shoes next to the California Zephyr at Grand Junction, Colorado. My parents likely were en route to Washington, D.C.

KEN THOMPSON

DAY TRIP TO WARNER BROS.

My mother Phyllis Merrill poses with me and my sister Marilyn in the backlot at Warner Bros. studios in 1953. The trip was part of a special tour arranged by Dad, Dick Merrill, a commercial artist who probably had a friend or two in the company's animation studio. We are dressed according to the standards of the day—heels and slim-silhouette day dress for Mom, and sneakers, bobby socks and full skirts for us girls.

JAY MERRILL FINLAY
SUN CITY WEST, AZ

STRIPES ARE IN

Mom did the packing for our trip to visit relatives in Ohio in 1953. She bought us three boys matching orange-and-brown striped shirts. We stayed overnight with our relatives, and when we all came down for breakfast, our two cousins were wearing the same shirts as ours! In the picture are our cousins Tom and Bill, then me and my brother Tom. My little brother, Keith, is in front.

DENNIS WENTZ · GUYS MILLS, PA

PEASANT DRESSES AND LEISURE SUITS

Here are members of my family in what I call the "Fashions of the '70s." The girls wear frilly peasant dresses and the boy sports a leisure suit—two styles popular in 1978, when this picture was taken.

ODETTE LANDERS
FORT PIERCE, FL

LOOKING SPIFFY

I was 7 when this was taken outside our family home in Walkerton, Indiana, on Easter Sunday 1947. Boys' dress hats were miniature versions of men's hats. Other popular hat styles for boys at the time were beanies, newsboy-style caps and brimmed straw hats.

RALPH SMITH · NEW ALBANY, IN

THE PLAID WAY

Bud Robinson and I enjoy each other's company here in about 1956, shortly after we were married. We met while we were still in high school. My plaid day dress, likely with a crinoline, is typical of the era.

MARTHA ROBINSON · FAYETTE, AL

Hawaiian Shirt

Celebrities and many others bought in to the new craze.

Chinese and Japanese tailors immigrating to the Hawaiian territory in the early 20th century were some of the first to sew loose-fitting men's shirts from bright kimono fabric. Bing Crosby endorsed the tropical style, and by the late 1930s, the shirts were fashionable as island souvenirs. U.S. service members returned from Pacific tours wearing the look, and a relaxed President Harry Truman on the cover of *Life* in 1951 gave the breezy style maximum exposure. Merriam-Webster added the definition the following year.

NATALIE WYSONG

With island attitude, Elvis plays the ukulele while wearing a Hawaiian shirt in 1961's *Blue Hawaii.*

Army test pilot F.W. Hunter sports aviator sunglasses at the Douglas Aircraft Co. plant in Long Beach, California, in 1942.

AVIATOR SUNGLASSES

OPTICAL SPECIALIST BAUSCH & LOMB INTRODUCED a tinted anti-glare lens for pilots in 1937. The thin teardrop frame gave wearers a wide field of vision—handy for fishing and golf, too. American Optical, among others, made millions of pairs for the military in the war years. Merriam-Webster added the term in 1944, the year Gen. Douglas MacArthur put aviators in the public eye when he wore them on his triumphant return to the Philippines. With everything military in fashion, civilians snapped up surplus sunglasses postwar, and aviators became a style mainstay.

NATALIE WYSONG

IN DEMAND

Military pilots did not wear Ray-Bans. Bausch & Lomb launched Ray-Bans as a civilian brand when the company realized it was on to something with its sunglasses.

The pixie was the "in" hairstyle for Toni, Helen and Melanie in 1967. Above, a Twiggified Toni.

Turning Out Twiggy

Supermodel obsession sweeps the block.

One hot afternoon in 1967 during summer vacation in Montgomery, Alabama, my sister, Melanie, brought home some magazines. Melanie was almost a teenager, but to 10-year-old me, she seemed grown up.

The magazines featured a doe-eyed model with pouty lips, a pixie haircut and a stick-thin figure. Intrigued, I pored through the pages. I was captivated by the high-fashion photos of this uber-thin girl/woman appropriately called Twiggy. I thought she was just completely darling.

I wanted to look just like Twiggy, and daydreamed about being her. I already had the straight figure—I was a skinny kid—and the blond hair. The next step, I decided, was to get a short haircut.

Mom was more than happy to oblige with permission for the haircut—she preferred my hair short anyway. Melanie, always the trailblazer, had already gotten her own chic pixie cut, and thoroughly enjoyed its coolness in the sweltering summer.

Off I went to the local beauty shop, where the hairdresser razor-cut my medium-length hair into a cropped pixie with a ducktail in the back. Going home, I felt like a real celebrity.

Aunt Martha, fun-loving and 22, loved my new hairstyle. She offered to add her own touches using makeup to help me get the look of my idol.

She brushed mascara on my eyelashes and told me not to blink. Then she applied generous amounts of lipstick and told me not to lick my lips. I was so worried about messing up my makeup by flickering my eyelids or licking my lips that I looked pretty peculiar—I had big unblinking eyes and fish lips!

As a finishing touch, Aunt Martha painted extra long eyelashes under my eyes to achieve the famous lashes we called Twiggies. Then I posed as Aunt Martha snapped photos with my Kodak Instamatic camera. Made up and with my new haircut, I had a few special hours of being Twiggy.

The next day, my friend from across the street, Helen Heckendorn, saw my new haircut and loved it so much that she got her own Twiggy cut. After that, we had tons of fun pretending we were Twiggy twins.

I was, of course, a far cry from the real thing, but it felt real enough to me, and we girls really enjoyed our summer vacation. In fact, the only one not enthusiastic about the makeover craze was Jim, my 6-year-old brother.

TONI BOOZER · OHATCHEE, AL

Bill's sweater still looks like new. Above, Helen and Bill Sr. are toasty at an outdoor rink.

OLD CRAFT
FOR A NEW LAND

HAVING IMMIGRATED TO CANADA FROM SCOTLAND in the spring of 1957, when I was 4, we had to adjust to many new things that we were not used to, including our first Canadian winter.

Although the winter season in Scotland was about the same length, it wasn't at all the same weather. Winter there was more damp than anything else. In Canada, we felt temperatures dipping to depths we'd never known. As the crisp fall air turned brisk that year, my mum, Helen, soon realized our outdoor clothing wasn't going to keep us warm. We were like early pioneers for our family; years later, more of our relatives would follow us to Canada. They would know from our experience how to prepare for the season.

Thankfully, Mum was a skilled knitter and set about making matching wool jackets for herself; my dad, Bill Sr.; and me. They featured designs resembling indigenous symbols on the front, back and sleeves. They certainly were eye-catching, especially when we all wore our jackets together.

I donated Mum's and Dad's jackets several years ago, but I kept mine as a cherished treasure of that first memorable winter season in our adopted country.

BILL SMILLIE JR. · GRIMSBY, ON

FOCUS ON:
COWICHAN SWEATER

Helen Smillie's jackets are in the style of Cowichan sweaters, which originated in the 19th century among the Cowichan people of British Columbia. By the '50s, their designs were so popular, imitations abounded, and yarn companies sold patterns for home knitters. In 2011, the Canadian government designated Cowichan artisans and sweaters as nationally significant. Vintage genuine Cowichan sweaters may cost about $200. New sweaters by Cowichan knitters can be found for around $400.

·················

John Glenn relaxed in a pair of Chucks on the USS *Noa* immediately after his Friendship 7 flight in 1962.

Cool Runnings

From gym court to punk-rock stage,
Chuck Taylors score a century of wins.

W hen Marquis Mills Converse devised his over-the-ankle sneaker in 1917, it wasn't a direct answer to a need in the marketplace. He had started Converse Rubber Co. nine years earlier in Malden, Massachusetts, making a variety of cold-weather rubber items, including galoshes and duck-hunting boots. But the business was only seasonal. Converse thought of making athletic shoes as a way of keeping his factory operating through the summer.

Those early shoes likely were designed with soccer and the basketball-like netball in mind. But around the time of the First World War, basketball was becoming popular in cities because it was a relatively compact game that could be played anywhere.

Converse's sneakers had features that seemed a good fit for basketball playing, including an ankle-hugging design. But sales were slow.

It wasn't until 1922, when an affable young basketball enthusiast from Columbus, Indiana, named Charles Hollis "Chuck" Taylor took a sales job at Converse, that the sneakers sold fast.

Converse All Stars were the world's bestselling basketball shoes before making an equally remarkable leap into the world of popular fashion. Today, they continue to enjoy special status as the footwear of cool rebels everywhere.

MARY-LIZ SHAW

New tones in 1971 were green, orange, light blue, navy, gold, off-white and red.

"Olympic white" Chuck Taylors. On a muddy outdoor court, the U.S. takes gold in a 19-8 win against Canada. Chucks remain the U.S. team's official shoe through the 1968 Games.

. . . .

1922

Taylor, above, a star of his high school basketball team, played for many semipro clubs beginning in 1919. The story goes that Taylor walked into the Chicago offices of Converse complaining of sore feet. In 1922, Converse hires him to promote its redesigned All Star line as a basketball shoe. Taylor is no ordinary salesman. He coaches the company's basketball team and runs clinics all over the country, developing close relationships with coaches and players, and highlighting their feats in annual Converse yearbooks.

. . . .

1932

Converse adds Chuck Taylor's signature to its All Star ankle patch. It solidifies his identity with the brand.

. . . .

1936

All Stars are named the official shoe of the U.S. basketball team at the Olympic Games. This is the first year the game is an Olympic sport and it marks the debut of Converse's

1957

Converse introduces its low-top Oxfords, which become popular as casual shoes off the court. That same year, kids on the new sitcom *Leave It to Beaver* wear Chuck Taylor low-tops under rolled-up jeans.

. . . .

1962

Wilt Chamberlain wears a pair of Chuck high-tops when he scores his record-setting 100 points in a single NBA game.

. . . .

1969

Calling him a basketball ambassador, the board of the Naismith Memorial Basketball Hall of Fame names Chuck Taylor to its class of 1969. He dies later that year.

. . . .

1971

Converse debuts Chucks in seven new colors, above, bolstering the brand's growing popularity among rock stars and in the counterculture.

2001

Despite the popularity of its Chuck line as a fashion shoe, Converse struggles to match the technical advances in athletic shoes of competitors. It declares bankruptcy.

. . . .

2003

Converse's one-time rival Nike buys the company for $315 million.

. . . .

2015

Nike sells an average of 270,000 pairs of Chuck Taylors a day.

The Sharks, led by Bernardo (George Chakiris), wear Chuck Taylor low-tops in *West Side Story* (1961).

Kippie Kovacs, the daughter of comedian Ernie Kovacs, poses in front of pinball machines in Virginia City, Nevada.

Pinball Flipout

Pop hands out nickels, and she conquers the playfield.

"Do you want to go to the arcade?" my grandfather asked one day in the summer of 1960. Pop, as we called him, didn't need to ask twice. I ran out to his Plymouth Belvedere as fast as my little 5-year-old legs could carry me.

It was a short ride to Leon's Arcade at the Long Branch Boardwalk. My older brother, Glenn, was already there with his friends, having ridden his bike to the pier. Leon's was always crowded and I stood with Pop at the entrance, drinking it in.

What a din! Music from the antique carousel swirled in the background, accompanied by the constant thud from the Skee-Ball machines. Most enticing were the clicking flippers, thumping bumpers, and chiming bells from the many pinball machines.

I watched intently as Glenn played on one of them, mesmerized by the colorful art on the playfield and backbox, as well as the deftness with which he controlled that little silver ball.

"Teach me to play!" I said. Glenn gave me a few pointers, but soon got tired of me hanging around. "Go play on your own—that's how you'll learn." I got a handful of nickels from Pop and dragged a soda crate to one of the machines.

I climbed up and played until the coins ran out. Pop smiled when I asked for more. The afternoon flew by while I tried machine after machine, until Pop finally said, "It's time to go now."

I played as often as I could at arcades all along the Jersey Shore. Sometimes I could wheedle Dad into renting a machine to put in our house for several weeks. That really boosted my popularity with the neighborhood kids!

My skills were put to the test in 1977 when I entered a pinball tournament at Monmouth College (now University) in West Long Branch while I was a student there. I was the only woman in the competition, and much to the chagrin of the guys in the game room, I bested the field and won a trophy.

Nowadays, you can often find my husband and me at the Silverball Museum Arcade in Asbury Park, where we have VIP memberships to indulge our mutual passion for pinball.

Whenever I see a youngster standing on a plastic step stool, flipping away, I can't help offering encouragement and a pointer: The more you play, the better you'll get.

CHERYL MILLER · OAKHURST, NJ

Chasing North Star

In the search for a game, Dad and son make a big discovery.

———

My father, Randy, often talked about how much he loved playing pinball at the arcade when he was growing up. Finding one of those games from his past always seemed like the ultimate gift for him, and when I finally learned the name of his favorite—North Star—I began my search.

A few weeks later, I found the North Pole-themed game through an online collector community, and my brother and I went to pick it up. As we loaded it into the truck, the seller said, "Just so you know, this won't be your last game." I didn't tell him it was a gift.

It was the first time I'd ever looked inside a pinball machine. I touched up the paint, restoring the game to its original luster, and got everything in perfect working order. We surprised Dad a few days before his birthday. He recognized the game when he saw the corner of the cabinet.

He stared in disbelief at the machine, which he hadn't seen in 50 years. I reminded him that he'd told me about North Star a few weeks earlier. He pressed the start button—the ding of the bells as the ball rolled through its first switch brought a huge smile to his face. After playing a few more balls, Dad stopped and said, "Now, did I ever tell you the name of my second-favorite pinball machine?"

That was a little over a year ago. Dad has seven machines now, including three that he played in the local arcade when he was a teenager in the late '60s. I've collected more than a dozen.

We enjoy this hobby, as well as the online communities of complete strangers willing to help one another. We're still hunting for Dad's elusive second favorite, Tropic Isle.

MICHAEL HALE · CAMBRIDGE SPRINGS, PA

Bumpers and bright colors are just part of the fun of playing pinball.

Lorraine daydreamed about living it up on the beach, like surfer girl Gidget.

West Coast Fling

Her heart was in the city all along.

A born and bred New Yorker, growing up in the Bronx, I've never wanted to live anywhere else, except for a brief period when Southern California called my name, thanks to the TV show *Gidget*.

The year was 1965 and I was 7. That same year, The Mamas & The Papas released "California Dreamin'" and like that my fantasy life had a soundtrack. I later doubled down on my wish to move to the West Coast when *The 4:30 Movie*, which aired weekday afternoons on Channel 7 WABC-TV, introduced me to more of the beach set, including Sandra Dee in the film version of *Gidget* and coastal couple Annette Funicello and Frankie Avalon.

That dream life was one where I did nothing but run on the sand to the ocean to hang 10. I'd float away from shore on a surfboard (after I waxed it according to the Beach Boys) and wait to catch a wave. I practiced by standing on an ironing board on my bed—luckily, I didn't crack my head open.

When my mother caught me in action and wanted to know what I was doing, the cleverest answer I could think of was "nothing." If she knew I was emulating my surfer-chick idols, she might have banned all beach-themed entertainment. A single mom who worked full time, she was too tired to probe, and told me only to return the ironing board to its proper place.

After that I scaled back on playing "pretend California," although my longing to shoot the curl at Big Sur lasted a few more years.

When I was about 10, my mother took me from our outer borough into Manhattan to see the Christmas Spectacular at Radio City Music Hall. The crowds, the glamour and the energy in the air as we emerged from the subway were a far cry from anything I'd experienced in the Bronx. That day began a new destination obsession—one I fulfilled with my husband, Neil, who's spent the last 40 years with me at home in New York City.

I'm glad, though, that at least for a little while, I was a Cali girl—if only in my mind.

LORRAINE MERKL · NEW YORK, NY

SURFER: NUTURE/GETTY IMAGES

Outfitted for Fun

That's me in 1946 in my much-cherished dudess outfit. My dad, Richard Merrill, took the picture outside our home in Oakland, California.

JAY MERRILL FINLAY · SUN CITY WEST, AZ

CHAPTER 5

....

AT
WORK

Whether supporting a family, paving the
way for others or working a summer job,
these storytellers speak to all of us.

Nancy's Seat

My father-in-law, Stan Tindall, works his cornfield with his daughter
Nancy, 3, beside him in a box on the tractor. This picture was
taken in the autumn of 1953. Nancy and I married 19 years later.

CECIL YODER · LE MARS, IA

Take the Greyhound to Chicago

Country girls find their calling in the city.

—

B orn in 1925 in a log cabin on my parents' farm in Thorp, Wisconsin, I was the fourth of a total of eight children. Our two-bedroom house didn't have electricity, running water or indoor plumbing.

All eight of us kids shared the farm chores. I was in charge of milking our six cows twice a day. It had to be done every morning before school and again in the evening, and Dad sold the milk locally. With my parents working in the fields, my grandmother, who lived with us, did most of the cooking for our family.

I got my first job when I was 15, working at Blue Moon cheese factory in Thorp. But I had higher ambitions and, in 1944, with my parents' blessing, my friend Valeria and I took the Greyhound bus from Thorp to Union Station in downtown Chicago. My cousin George picked us up.

Valeria and I moved in with my relatives, who lived on the southwest side of Chicago in the Brighton Park neighborhood. George took quite a liking to Valeria.

I began to look for a job right away. The city was bustling, a big change from the pace of our serene farm town, and World War II was in full

Dodge Chicago hired women to assemble Wright Cyclone engines for B-29 bombers in 1944. Small-town friends Valeria, above left, and Lucille moved to the big city.

owing. I found work on the South Side at the Dodge plant, which hired female factory workers to assemble Wright Cyclone engines for the B-29 bombers being sent to the front.

The positions that performed the final testing of the engines required a college degree, but with college graduates in short supply, I got a promotion. I was trained to use a slide rule and how to determine whether or not engines met full specifications.

That career ended abruptly one day when word spread throughout the plant that the war had ended. Everyone simply got up and left their workstations, never to return to those jobs. We quietly headed out to the streets, where people were cheering and celebrating.

I found another job at Motorola Corp., working on the assembly line under the eye of a strict supervisor. At times, I assembled more than 1,000 televisions per day as they came down the line, with barely time to wipe my nose. I remained at that job until I retired many years later.

In the meantime, George and Valeria got married, and I became acquainted with Steve Wojtowicz after he returned home at the end of the war. He'd served overseas, both in France with Gen. George Patton's 3rd Army, and at the Battle of the Bulge. My friends and family teased me about being in a serious relationship after he wooed me with flowers on my birthday. He'd proudly carried the huge bouquet on the bus all the way to my house. We got married in Thorp on a scorching hot July day in 1947, and shared 55 happy years together.

LUCILLE WOJTOWICZ · CHICAGO, IL

Back in the Black

Airman is under orders to shape up the officers' club.

O

ne year remained in my four-year stint as an Air Force captain when I unexpectedly had to leave my wife and two small children behind in Columbia, South Carolina, in 1971 and report for duty at Nakhon Phanom Royal Thai Air Force Base in Thailand. Despite zero experience, I was put in charge of turning around operations for the officers' club, which had a bar, a liquor store, slot machines and a restaurant that served more than 1,000 meals a day. Open 24 hours a day, seven days a week, the club was losing $30,000 a month.

My staff consisted of Sgt. Williams, known as Willie, who was my saving grace, and 160 Thai employees, including a young and talented chef. I left the club in Willie's hands while I read reams of Air Force regulations governing labor and goods costs, pricing, staffing standards, sanitation and so on. Pam, the office manager and one of only two

Thai employees who spoke English, also helped keep the club afloat while I got my sea legs.

I identified several reasons the club was operating in the red: Some items, such as meat, were required to be purchased and shipped from the U.S., and the prices of local staples, such as produce, were unexpectedly high. We constantly had to replace silverware and dishes. Shipments of items such as apples disappeared before ever reaching the tables. And the slot machines, which were being phased out, were mysteriously losing money.

The club purchased most of its vegetables, fruit, rice and other staples locally from Sui-Thai, a businessman who worked with many of the American bases. He drove a 1930s convertible with machine guns strapped, gangster-style, inside the doors. His prices were inflated and he casually displayed his guns if anyone mentioned

At far left are office staff with Capt. Hartzog, center, and Pam, office supervisor, to his left. Capt. Hartzog stands at a meal with fellow officers at near left. Above, Sgt. Williams, left, is with the club chef.

negotiation. Somehow I survived bucking his system, and we found much cheaper goods with other suppliers.

Strangely enough, a local contractor paid us for the privilege of picking up our garbage each day. After I learned we bought our silverware and dinnerware from this same contractor, I deduced that he had an arrangement with busboys to drop forks, spoons and dishes into the garbage, which were then retrieved and sold back to the club.

Apples were not available in Thailand, and every time we received a shipment of them, the workers smuggled them out, hidden in their bras, underwear and socks. In the village, apples could fetch up to $5 each, whereas the average wage for the workers was 5 cents per hour. I began giving one apple to every worker and set consequences for being caught with an unauthorized apple.

Most of the coins put into the slot machines ended up in the pockets of the technicians who serviced them. Once we corrected that, the gaming profit skyrocketed, even as we continued to phase out the machines.

I did a survey to find out why more officers didn't come to the club, and based on the results, we introduced theme nights, special menus and contests. Business picked up, along with income, as we engaged bands and hired a dancer, a superstar who packed the bar every night—that is, until an officer whose tour was up took her to the U.S. and married her.

So many other stories came out of that incredible year. When we could not get butter or margarine for several weeks, we got many complaints. One day, Willie showed me a platter of perfectly formed patties of butter! He'd mixed lard with salt, flavoring and yellow food coloring, and cut the cooled mixture into patties. Initially, it got good reviews, but it wasn't long before the suggestion box began to have notes such as "Thank you for finding butter to serve again. However, it tastes like lard and sticks to the roof of my mouth."

In preparation for a huge sanitation inspection, we trained the staff in the required stringent procedures. Moments before the inspectors arrived, I was dismayed to find the dishwashing staff running their dirty socks through the conveyor belt for washing dishes—an established routine that hadn't been covered in the training for the inspection.

I also learned that one of the workers in the club was a general from the exiled Laotian army who'd disguised himself as a carpenter.

When my tour in Thailand was up, the club had gone from losing money each month to making a profit, even with giving up the slot machines. I was awarded the Air Force Commendation Medal for my work, a real honor. And I'd made 160 new Thai friends.

ART HARTZOG · CHESNEE, SC

Trailblazing Teacher

Education is the theme in this centenarian's life.

Edith Smith is one of the many wonderful people I met during my 39 years of teaching public school in Chicago. I was 22, and had started teaching at the brand-new Ludwig Van Beethoven Elementary School at 47th and State streets on Chicago's South Side in 1962.

The new school quickly grew overcrowded, and within a few weeks, I had 48 third graders. The principal opened additional classroom space in the nearby Robert R. Taylor Homes public housing project and a park district building, and hired Edith Smith, who had master teacher certification.

Edith retired in 1976 after teaching for more than two decades, and continued to volunteer for many years. Having learned some of her remarkable life story during that time, I contacted *Chicago Sun-Times* columnist Neil Steinberg, who interviewed her shortly before her 107th birthday in July 2021.

Edith Renfrow was born in 1914 in Grinnell, Iowa. Her father, Lee, was a chef at the Monroe Hotel. Edith's grandparents, George and Eliza Jane Craig, were born into slavery. Her grandfather, who came from Virginia, was the son of a slave owner; her grandmother, born in South Carolina, was separated from her mother when she was only a child and sent to live in freedom in Ohio.

Edith was the fifth of six children, all of whom went to college. She enrolled at Grinnell College, and was the first African American woman to graduate in 1937. Jobs were scarce when she moved to Chicago, but she found work at the YWCA and later at the University of Chicago, before becoming a teacher in the public schools.

Grinnell College awarded her an honorary doctorate in 2019, the same year the Edith Renfrow Smith '37 Black Women's Library opened on campus.

Edith celebrated her 100th birthday in 2014 by buying a new fiery red Fiat 500. She told me she had to sell it after she injured her wrist—she could no longer make left turns.

GREG LOPATKA · DOWNERS GROVE, IL

Edith Smith holds a portrait from a family scrapbook.

Wilcox brothers Dewell, left, and Max stand with the International truck piled high.

On the Road with Dad

Daughter has a long wait for a hamburger.

My dad, Max Wilcox, and his brother Dewell were short-haul truck drivers. Dad drove his 1941 International truck from our home in Albuquerque to Gallina, where he picked up rough green lumber and brought it back to Albuquerque to sell to Duke City Lumber Co.

Gallina was 110 miles away on dirt roads that made it hard going when it rained. During the summer, Dad sometimes hauled two loads in a day. In the winter, if he got stuck, he'd try to find a nearby house where he could spend the night and wait for the ground to freeze. If he couldn't get out in the morning, the truck had to be unloaded and dug out.

My brother sometimes rode along, but Dad didn't think a sawmill was safe for me, a 6-year-old in 1946. My brother told me all about stopping for lunch—I'd never had a hamburger or a Coke, much less been in a cafe. I begged to go along.

One evening at bedtime, Dad told me tomorrow was the day. He woke me at 3:30 in the morning. I put on my dress, anklets and oxford shoes, and soon we were on the road. We were well out of Albuquerque before the sun came up. I looked out the window at the hills and fields of wildflowers—yellow, white and purple—which are all gone now.

At the busy sawmill, Dad backed his truck under a load of lumber. I stayed in the truck while he went into the office to pay. Suddenly, there was a loud bang and I was bounced up inside the cab, hitting my head. The mill workers had released the load of lumber onto the truck.

On the way home, we stopped at the cafe, where we sat on stools at the counter. The waitress asked, "What will you have?" Dad said, "I think she wants an ice cream cone." For a moment, I was disappointed, then Dad laughed and said, "Naw, you better make it a hamburger and Coke for this little lady."

It was the best meal I'd ever had.

Back in the truck, I lay down on the seat and slept all the way home.

HELEN BURSON · ALBUQUERQUE, NM

Don piloted the Airbus A320, shown here behind him in Grand Cayman Island in 2017.

Identical jackets and bow ties made Don and Ron the center of attention on their flight in 1965.

Instruments of Destiny

In the cockpit, 8-year-old sees his future.

For our first flight, from Miami, Florida, to Memphis, Tennessee, my identical twin brother, Ron, and I wore matching Sunday dress clothes—even our bow ties were the same. It was the summer of 1965 and we were 8.

The flight attendants made a fuss about us being identical twins, but my interest was someplace else—the cockpit! The captain saw me straining my neck to get a peek at all those knobs and switches as we stepped into the DC-8, and he invited us inside the compartment. At that time, it took three pilots to fly a DC-8: a captain, a first officer and an engineer. I was fascinated with what I saw, and from that moment all I wanted was to learn how to fly an airplane.

We eventually had to take our seats in the cabin, but I can't remember if we flew in first class or coach that day, because my mind was still up there with the captain.

I am proud to say I went on to get my pilot's license—even before my driver's license—and have been flying ever since. I currently fly the Boeing 777, and one of my favorite things is watching children's faces light up when my fellow pilots and I invite them to visit the cockpit. Each time we do this, I remember my first flight and hope I am leaving them with a lifelong impression.

That is the case with my two boys, Geoff and Greg. The Army has chosen Geoff to fly the Black Hawk helicopter, and Greg is a charter pilot.

After 32 years with American Airlines, I'll be retiring soon. As I taxi down the runway out of Miami headed to Europe or South America, I know my time piloting these magnificent machines is coming to an end. Thankfully, my days of travel will continue with my wife, Diane, hopefully for years to come.

DONALD MASHBURN · VERO BEACH, Fl

WORLD OF TOMORROW—TODAY!

Technology promises a gleaming horizon.

« 1950

All Business
After the breakthrough of the Mark I computer in 1944, IBM focused on faster machines for commercial use. Its swirling red loops forming an atom, this ad promotes vacuum-tube computers, which became payroll and inventory workhorses for big companies by the end of the '50s.

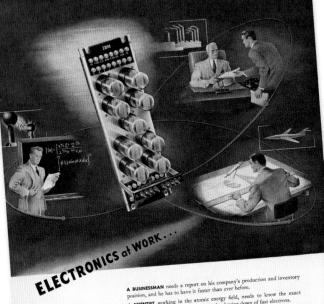

1958 »

Signaling a Change
With space and long-distance communications captivating American culture in the 1950s, Pontiac puts a young couple and a snazzy Super Chief next to a massive radar antenna—a symbol of progress for "a bold new generation."

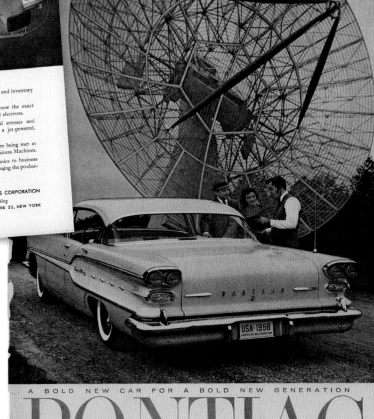

Lifestyles of the Future Rich & Famous

The airplane represented the pinnacle of new society in postwar America. At top, a Douglas Aircraft Co. ad, touting the new DC-6 plane design, uses modernist-style graphics repeated across the page to convey the company's global reach. Above, an eye-catching spot in the "Fresh From Motorola" print series of the early '60s features a couple relaxing in an ultramodern window-walled space reminiscent of the famous Stahl house in Los Angeles.

HIGH POINT
A worker stands next to the canoe beams that will brace the viewing deck of Seattle's Space Needle. It took about 400 days to build the structure for its debut at the World's Fair in 1962.

What this Teacher Did on Summer Vacation

Temp job wrestling hams gets an F.

People think teachers have it easy with summers off. But as a young teacher with a family and a mortgage, I couldn't afford to be unemployed for three months.

In 1977, Ann, a fellow teacher, suggested I check out Vernon, an industrial town near Los Angeles where her son had worked a meat-packing job.

"Great," I said. "If I can pack ideas into kids' minds, I can surely pack hot dogs into containers."

The plant manager, wearing a clean butchers coat, met me on my first day: "Put on your bump hat and follow me."

"Bump hat?"

"It'll protect your head if something hits it."

Ollie, the foreman, got me started lifting slippery, fatty 3- to-4-pound hams onto a conveyor belt. I tried not to drop any. After break, I moved on to packing the 7- to-10-pounders. Soon my hands, arms and back ached.

"Ham steaks are next," Ollie said. "Put a piece of plastic on each one. If you miss any, the machine stops until you catch up." The belt stopped many times during my shift. How could a simple job be so hard?

At home, my wife greeted me holding her nose. "Whoa, you stink!"

I went to bed early and dreamed of pigs.

On my second day, it was harder to hold on to the hams. When I dropped one, I washed it off before putting it back on the conveyor. "Every time you drop a ham, you cut into profits," Ollie said. "Don't wash the hams unless the federal inspector is around."

My faith in the hygienic practices of the plant was shattered, but I put my aching muscles into high gear, trying to work faster and send only clean hams to market. Finally, exhausted, I stopped.

I found Ollie and tapped him on the shoulder, interrupting his tirade at a worker. "Ollie, old man, I quit. How do I get out of here?"

Ollie pointed at my head. "You have to give back your bump hat."

I worked two other jobs that summer, one in a bra factory and one in a produce warehouse. I even got a day to bask on the beach and one to take my son fishing.

RICHARD HULSE · OXNARD, CA

The Dacotah Street School faculty softball team poses in 1977, Richard is at right with the ball.

Ivan takes in the view during a water break. At left, Camp Independence is shown with the laundry tent in the foreground.

A Season at Camp Independence

U.S. Forest Service workers restore land in Idaho.

The summer of 1966, I worked for the U.S. Forest Service in north central Idaho's Clearwater National Forest.

I found a ride from North Carolina with a college student who needed passengers on a trip to California. Stopping only for food and gas, we traveled to Salt Lake City, Utah, where I began to make my way to the Forest Service office in Pierce, Idaho. After a short orientation, 25 or so of us workers were on our way to our summer home, Camp Independence.

The camp was mostly tents. We slept four to a tent, each of which had a wood stove—one of our tasks was cutting and gathering wood—and a light powered by a generator, which shut down at 10 p.m.

After breakfast, we got a ride to our work sites. I was armed with a hoedag, a short-handled hatchet with a prong at one end, to dig out and destroy the roots of currant plants, varieties of which cause disease in white pine trees. Generally I worked alone. At noon, a distant voice called out "Lunch!" and I sat down with the sack lunch I'd packed. A half-hour later, the call came to return to work.

The job paid $2.05 an hour, and we were charged $1.15 for each of our three daily meals. A few workers quit, but for those who stayed, there were weekend hikes into the mountains, which had black bears, moose, deer and snow. Sometimes we caught a ride over the Bitterroot Mountains through Hoodoo Pass to Superior, Montana.

In August, I bought a 1957 Chevy station wagon from a fellow worker. I took three workmates with me to help pay for the trip back home. I dropped off two passengers in Oklahoma and one in Mississippi. With the cost of car repairs on the way back to North Carolina, I didn't bank much money, but I made so many memories that I can scarcely recall them all.

IVAN NICHOLSON · BEMIDJI, MN

The Bellavigna brothers mind the store in 1949 or '50. At top right, Edward holds 18-month-old Richard in 1952.

Neighborhood Mom & Pop

Brothers make J&E Food Market into a local hub.

M y dad, Edmondo (Edward) Bellavigna, mustered out of the Army after his assignment to the Territory of Alaska, and in 1949 he and his older brother Giuseppe (Joseph) opened a store.

J&E Food Market was on Third Avenue and 50th Street, under the elevated Gowanus Parkway, in the Sunset Park area of Brooklyn. Their pop, Alfredo, an immigrant from Ancona, Italy, built all the wooden shelving for the store.

Dad and Uncle Joe made breakfast and lunch for the longshoremen who unloaded ships on the Brooklyn docks. Policemen, firemen and sanitation workers also were frequent customers.

We lived in an apartment above the market. When it was Dad's turn to work late, he'd bring me downstairs with him. One night, a customer ordered cold cuts, which Dad had to get from

the rear of the store. He left me up front by the cash register and cigarette racks. When Dad returned, I said, "He took fits!" (my 2-year-old's word for cigarettes).

Dad had the guy open his jacket—hidden inside were two packs of Lucky Strikes. Dad and my mom, Josephine, joked that I was the market's first security guard.

Growing up, I worked without pay, but I was allowed all I could eat from the store. Years later, Dad admitted that putting me on the payroll would have been cheaper.

After we moved out of the upstairs apartment and into a house in Bay Ridge, I continued to stock shelves and make deliveries. When I took on more responsibility, sometimes working six days a week, I complained about the $35 a week I got paid.

"This is what Joe and I got when we started," Dad said. Of course that was in 1949—it was now 1966.

J&E Food Market served that community for almost 25 years, extending credit to those who needed it. The customers' roots were from everywhere—Puerto Rico, Norway, China, Ireland, Italy, and countries in Africa—and the store was a gathering place for friends and family.

All these years later, a deli-grocery store is still at that location. Not a day goes by that I don't think fondly of the old market.

RICHARD BELLAVIGNA · BROOKLYN, NY

ONE-STOP SHOP

My mother-in-law, Juanita's, father—wearing white shoes—was part owner of this combo barbershop, cigar store, pool hall and card room. It was across from Union Station in Kansas City, Missouri, in the late 1920s. Juanita remembers driving to the shop with her mom to pick up her dad on Saturday nights.
RON SWANSON
SONORA, CA

Merci, Madame Myers

School reshuffle comes with a silver lining.

Small school districts across Kansas were consolidating when I was in grade school in the late 1960s. Buildings closed, district lines were redrawn and people expressed strong opinions about it all.

My first day as a seventh grader at my new school in Fairview was long and dull, until I met Madame Myers. She surprised us with the news that, every day, she would drive from nearby Hiawatha High School to teach us French.

Her lessons using songs, maps and games opened a new world. Mme Myers invited us to try reading one of her "real" French books. I struggled through *La Symphonie Pastorale* by André Gide, just barely following the plot. On my book report, which was in English, Mme Myers wrote *"très bien!"* This was lavish praise, as my paper was not even half good, but I was proud when I showed my parents.

When I went on to Hiawatha High School, I studied French with Mme Myers for another three years. Though no senior-level class was available for my fourth year, she still greeted me in the hallways with a *"Bonjour, mademoiselle!"*

After high school, I married a farmer. I sang French songs to our baby as I rocked him to sleep, and checked out the few French books that were in our public library.

In the agriculturally painful 1980s, our farming days ended, and we moved to Hollister, Missouri, where I began to attend college. Years had passed since my French classes, but Mme Myers had prepared me well, and I built on her lessons to earn my own certification to teach French.

When I need encouragement to navigate something new, I remember the change that brought Mme Myers. A quote by philosopher Albert Camus reminds me of her. Translated, it means "In the midst of winter, I found there was, within me, an invincible summer."

CAROL SPANGLER · FAIRVIEW, KS

Carol smiles in 1964, a few years before she began to learn French.

A toy can become a tool for the future, if you play it right.

Driven to Success

His grandfather had his back.

Back in July 1958, my grandparents—Memere and Pepere—gave me a red and silver pedal-powered tractor for my fifth birthday. That Christmas, Pepere built me a single-axle trailer to match it. The tractor was my favorite toy, and I'm sure it made them happy that I enjoyed their gift so much.

One day in the summer of 1959, I was riding around the driveway when out of the blue I decided to back the trailer into the walkway. I became very frustrated that the trailer would not go where I aimed it.

Pepere happened to be there and saw my dilemma. He offered instruction and advice. He owned a boat and trailer, so he knew the trick of it.

I then spent many hours that day and the next practicing backing up that little trailer to where I wanted it to go until I mastered it.

Many years later, when I was in my early 20s, I decided what I wanted to do in life. I enrolled in truck school and began my career as a tractor-trailer driver. I have often wondered if on that day when Pepere helped me with that little tractor and trailer, he planted a seed that led to my lifelong job driving big trucks all over New England.

Sadly, Pepere did not live long enough to see that happen. But over the years, I occasionally pictured him looking down on me backing a rig into a dock and telling his friends, "That's my grandson driving," and then describing how he helped me one day when I was just a boy playing in the yard.

There is a saying: If you like your job, then you're not really working. Pepere, thank you!

DAVID INGRAM · NORTH BROOKFIELD, MA

Making History

One woman paves the way for others with her career.

As astronaut John Glenn prepared for America's first crewed orbit around the Earth in 1962, he wasn't willing to trust the early electronic computers. "Get the girl to check the numbers," he said of their go-to mathematician. "I was that girl," Katherine Johnson said many years later. She would also become known as part of NASA's untold story—included in the *Hidden Figures* book and movie—of the Black women who contributed to the space program's success.

Her parents put education first. Katherine was the youngest of Joshua and Joylette Coleman's four children. The couple moved when no grade school was open to Black children in their area of West Virginia—and moved again when there was no high school for them.

A gifted student, she skipped whole grades. Katherine started high school at 10. She graduated from high school at 14 and from college at 18.

Johnson wanted to be a research mathematician but could not find that kind of work as a woman of color. After years of raising a family and teaching, she got her chance in 1953, joining the National Advisory Committee for Aeronautics, the forerunner of NASA at the Langley Research Center. She worked there for 33 years, into the shuttle era.

Women were long hired as mathematicians for the department, freeing the male engineers from time-consuming calculations. And she was a human computer.

The movie *Hidden Figures* is mostly accurate. Johnson did work in a segregated "colored" group, but she never used a separate bathroom—first, because she didn't realize the bathroom she used was intended only for whites, and later, because she ignored the sign.

A NASA building is among the structures named in her honor. At 97, she received the Presidential Medal of Freedom from President Barack Obama—and a kiss on the cheek from the person she had proudly voted for.

AMY RABIDEAU SILVERS

Katherine Johnson (1918-2020) attained her NASA dream job.

"I liked what I was doing. I liked work. I liked the stars, and the stories we were telling."

Express Pony

In 1968, my parents said I could have a horse if I bought it myself.
I'm sure they thought it would never happen, but I did save enough
from my paper route to buy the most beautiful mare.

SANDY SMITH WILLIAMS · ENOREE, SC

CHAPTER 6

OUR
HEROES

Read touching personal accounts from those who proudly served our country and from those who knew them best.

Kumhwa Valley Strike

As a 21-year-old Army rifle squad leader (back row, right), I was responsible for nine infantrymen. Near the end of winter in 1952 we were conducting border patrols in the Kumhwa Valley in Korea. Suddenly, we came under a fierce mortar attack. We lost our medic, Cpl. Finny. I retrieved his bag of medical supplies and tended to the wounded. We were able to radio our location for air support and, within minutes, Navy jets struck the North Korean position, giving us time to evacuate.

RAY RICHMOND · CYPRESS, CA

LEFT: USA C-4626, ARMY SIGNAL CORPS COLLECTION, U.S. NATIONAL ARCHIVES NAVAL HISTORY

Historic Day on the Mighty Mo

Marine is on deck at the official end of World War II.

M y father, Edwin, was waiting his turn at the barbershop in 1965, browsing an *American Legion Magazine* article that chronicled the 20th anniversary of the end of World War II. A photograph showed thousands of sailors and Marines on the deck of a battleship, watching the treaty ceremony that marked the end of World War II.

Dad identified himself as the young Marine crouching in one corner of the shot and looking back at the camera. A Russian photographer behind him had dropped his camera, causing Dad to turn around.

Dad is in more than one of the photographs from the day the treaty was signed, including the photo here, which is taken from the same angle as the picture he saw in 1965. Dad is the Marine with the patch on his uniform.

Dad's assignment on the USS *Missouri* gave him the chance to witness this event firsthand. During

At left, brothers Billy and Edwin pose in uniform.

Edwin stands with hands clasped behind his back on the deck of the USS *Missouri*.

Both Edwin and Billy were in the South Pacific, but they were not aware of each other's location.

WWII, Dad enlisted in the Marine Corps several months after his older brother, Billy, joined. Both Edwin and Billy were in the South Pacific, but they were not aware of each other's location.

Assigned to a 50-person Marine detachment on the *Missouri*, which was nicknamed the Mighty Mo, Dad was part of some critical battles, including the invasion of Iwo Jima.

The *Missouri* also hosted the official surrender of the Japanese on Sept. 2, 1945. A 19-year-old Marine Corps corporal, Dad served as an honor guard to Lt. Gen. Kuzma Derevyanko, who represented the Soviet Union at the ceremony. Dad was 20 feet behind Gen. Douglas MacArthur during the signing of the peace treaty.

On Sept. 8, six days after the war ended, the battleship was en route to New York City for a Navy Day celebration when it made a refueling stop on the island of Guam.

Billy was there, and having learned in a letter from their parents that his brother was on the *Missouri*, he ran to the dock and got word to the crew to contact Edwin.

After being separated for more than a year, the brothers were reunited and spent the afternoon together on the beach. Billy wrote about the reunion to their parents back home in Arrow, Idaho.

GREG ASIMAKOUPOULOS · MERCER ISLAND, WA

Eugene Obregon is a source of civic pride in East L.A., where parks, a school, a highway and a monument to Latino medal-winners bear his name.

Brotherhood in Battle

Private selflessly shields a comrade.

Two days after his 17th birthday, my uncle Bert Johnson joined the Marine Corps. After boot camp, Bert was sent to Korea, where he became friends with Eugene Obregon. The two young men came from entirely different backgrounds but were the same age. Bert was from the small farm town of Grand Prairie, Texas; Eugene grew up in Los Angeles, California.

Bert and Eugene were fighting together during an assault on the city of Seoul. Eugene, who served as an ammunition carrier for a machine-gun squad, saw Bert fall. Eugene ran to his friend and dragged him to the side of the road, where he shielded Bert as he bandaged his wounds. Shooting with only a pistol as the enemy advanced, Eugene was killed by machine-gun fire.

After several months in the hospital, Bert returned to duty. In August 1951, he attended a ceremony to honor Eugene in Washington, D.C. Eugene's parents were there to accept the Medal of Honor for their only son.

After the ceremony, Bert visited the Grace Reformed Church, where a Marine Corps photographer took his picture, solemn as he stood in his uniform holding a lighted candle. Later, Bert's family was surprised to see that picture of him made into the 1951 Marine Corps Christmas poster. It was displayed in the Grand Prairie post office with an accompanying Bible verse: "Greater love hath no man than this, that a man lay down his life for his friends."

JAMES PARKER · ARLINGTON, TX

Parallel Paths

Marine's valor touches a childhood friend.

Lee Roy Herron and I met in the seventh grade at Matthews Junior High School in Lubbock, Texas. His parents, like mine, valued education as the primary means for their children to better themselves.

Lee Roy and I became fast friends, rivals in spelling bees and sports. We both played on the high school football team. In the fall of 1962, in the shadow of the Cuban missile crisis, we knew we would soon register for the draft.

Our college life began in 1963 at Texas Technological College, now Texas Tech University. Lee Roy joined the Marine Corps Platoon Leaders Course, training near Quantico, Virginia, in 1964. On his advice, I joined the Marine Corps in 1965, the year that President Johnson sent troops to Vietnam. We graduated in June 1967, two of only four graduates to receive Marine Corps second lieutenant commissions.

In February 1968 I was in the law program, preparing to serve as a Marine judge advocate, when Lee Roy called with the exciting news that he'd been selected to attend the Defense Language Institute Foreign Language Center to learn to be a Vietnamese translator. He was also getting married. In the middle of taking final exams, I was unable to attend Lee Roy's wedding. Missing that event is one of my deepest regrets.

Lee Roy died in Vietnam on Feb. 22, 1969. I knew little about what happened, beyond that he had stepped in to take the place of a wounded officer, confronted the enemy and was killed.

Decades later, I attended a speech by Marine Corps Col. Wesley Fox, one of my former instructors. I nearly fell out of my chair when he told of the heroic action of a man from West Texas: Lee Roy Herron.

Lee Roy was part of a company that came under attack while on patrol in the A Shau

Lee Roy Herron completed The Basic School for Marine Corps officers in 1968.

Valley, a densely forested region near South Vietnam's border with Laos.

Taking command after an officer was severely wounded, Lee Roy stirred the platoon to action, directing an assault against two enemy machine guns. He charged one of the bunkers under heavy cloud cover, scoring a direct hit. But the weather cleared while he prepared to go after the second bunker. In plain view, he was killed. With clearer conditions, company commander Fox called in air support to destroy the bunker. For his valor, Lee Roy was posthumously awarded the Navy Cross.

DAVID NELSON · HOUSTON, TX

The Speed Queen

Pilot breaks sound and other barriers.

When Jackie Cochran set her mind to something, she usually got her way. Her moxie helped the young Florida woman from an impoverished background land a job at a swanky New York salon. And it put her in the path of Floyd Odlum, a rich financier who advised her to learn to fly to build the cosmetics career she was starting.

Odlum offered her a deal: If she could earn her pilot's license in six weeks, he'd pay for it. Cochran did it in three, receiving her license Aug. 17, 1932.

Along with building her cosmetics business (slogan: Wings to Beauty), Cochran began competing in air races. By the end of the 1930s, she was setting speed and altitude records and winning recognition for aerial excellence.

With war in Europe on the horizon, Cochran advocated for American women to be trained to fly in non-combat roles. When the U.S. military didn't take her up on the offer, Cochran took several licensed female aviators to join the war effort in England, where civilian pilots were allowed to ferry aircraft to where they were needed.

Back home, a similar program developed. In 1943 Cochran became director of the Army's Women Airforce Service Pilots (WASP), which tested planes and logged flying time with new engines. But WASP's days were numbered: When male pilots began returning from combat duty in 1944, the program was disbanded. Cochran was awarded the Distinguished Service Medal for her leadership.

Cochran was, among other firsts, the first woman to fly faster than the speed of sound and the first to land and take off from an aircraft carrier. By the end of her long career, Jackie Cochran had earned three Distinguished Flying Crosses.

NATALIE WYSONG

Cochran stands on the wing of her F-86, talking with flying ace Chuck Yeager and chief test pilot Bill Longhurst.

Lawrence Joel was the first medic to earn the Medal of Honor during the Vietnam War.

Mission to Save Lives

Wounded medic carries on with his duties.

Lawrence Joel was born in 1928 in Winston-Salem, North Carolina, the third of 16 children. At 18, he joined the Army, serving his initial three-year enlistment in Europe.

A few years later, Joel signed up again, serving as an airborne medic in Lebanon and Alaska. In 1964 the seasoned veteran joined the 1st Battalion, 503rd Infantry Division, 173rd Airborne Brigade, the first major Army unit deployed to Vietnam.

The first several months in Vietnam were fairly quiet, with no sustained combat. That changed in early November 1965, when Joel was part of an operation that went on patrol to search for Viet Cong in the jungles near the city of Bien Hoa.

A battle began when the patrol walked into an ambush. Greatly outnumbered, the lead squad suffered heavy casualties in the initial burst of fire. Joel was shot in the leg, but he patched his own wound and gave himself a dose of morphine, then ran forward to administer care to the many wounded soldiers.

Joel was hit in the leg once more during the long firefight, which went on for more than 24 hours.

Using a makeshift crutch, the aidman moved from soldier to soldier, treating injuries and offering encouragement.

Joel spent three months recovering from his injuries. He received the Silver Star and a Purple Heart, and, in 1967, President Johnson presented him with the Medal of Honor.

Joel died in 1984 and is buried in Arlington National Cemetery.

NATALIE WYSONG

Hero in the Netherlands

Paratrooper gives his life for fellow soldiers.

My uncle Joe E. Mann was born on a wheat farm in eastern Washington and grew up in a big family. In August 1942, Joe enlisted in the Army, becoming a paratrooper in the 502nd Parachute Infantry Regiment, 101st Airborne Division. He trained at Toccoa, Georgia, the home of the regiment made famous by the war drama *Band of Brothers*. Joe also trained at Fort Benning, Georgia; Fort Bragg, North Carolina; and in England.

At some point during his training, Joe sent his mother a photo of himself in civilian clothes, standing next to a young woman. He identified the woman only as his fiancee, without giving her name. No one in our family ever got the chance to meet her.

On Sept. 17, 1944, Joe parachuted into the Netherlands as part of Operation Market Garden. The next day, with his platoon outnumbered and surrounded, Joe singlehandedly destroyed a German ammunition supply point and an 88 mm gun. Firing from an exposed position, Joe was struck multiple times.

Sent to shelter in a trench that held other wounded men, Joe was patched up, with his arms bandaged tightly against his body. He left the shelter of the trench and returned to the front line, where he stood guard so his buddies could sleep.

The next morning, the Germans attacked, throwing stick grenades that GIs called potato mashers. One fell next to Joe. Unable to use his arms, he threw himself on it. His final action saved the lives of six men.

Wings spread, the pelican atop this memorial for Joe Mann in Best, Netherlands, represents the mythical bird that sacrificed herself to save her babies.

For his heroism over that two-day period, Joe was posthumously awarded the Medal of Honor, the Bronze Star and five Purple Hearts.

Our family has long wondered whether Joe's unnamed fiancee ever learned that he was recognized as a hero in the Netherlands, with monuments built in his honor. Joe's nieces and nephews would still like to learn the identity of the aunt they never had.

BYRNE BENNETT · REARDAN, WA

VALOR IN ACTION

Medal of Honor
For this highest award for valor, a recipient's action must be verified by a witness. The Medal of Honor is the only combat-specific award that is worn around the neck.

....

Service Cross
Second only to the Medal of Honor, a service cross recognizes bravery in combat. Service crosses are specific to each branch of the military.

....

Silver Star
Originally called the Citation Star, this award was established in 1918 and bears the inscription "For gallantry in action."

....

Distinguished Flying Cross
Civilians as well as members of the military are eligible to receive this award for heroism and distinction in flight.

....

Bronze Star
This award for bravery in combat or for meritorious service can be awarded to both foreign military troops and American service members.

....

Purple Heart
Given to those wounded or killed in action, the Purple Heart bears the likeness of Gen. George Washington, who established an early form of the badge.

DOING WITHOUT

World War II was not a time for
a new refrigerator.

1943

Change in Production

Steel and other
materials used for
appliances were
sacrificed for the war
effort. By awaiting a
new refrigerator design
from Norge, this ad
says, you too will help
"speed the day of
Victory and Peace."

FIGHTING FORCE

SAFE HARBOR

My mother Doris holds me in a photo booth in Pawtucket, Rhode Island, in 1944. Our family briefly reunited with Dad in 1945 in San Francisco, California, while the destroyer he served on was under repair. After an exhausting train trip home to Pawtucket, with me at 10 months old, Mom was immediately told "The war is over."

ARTHUR LEON LOWTHER JR.
JACKSONVILLE, FL

SOLDIER IN FRANCE

I never knew Grandpa Al to travel outside of the U.S. But after he died, I learned that in 1943, after completing basic training at Fort Knox, Kentucky, the rifleman was sent overseas. He was wounded three times on his way from Italy to southern France in 1945, earning a Purple Heart with two oak-leaf clusters, before coming home to Edna in 1946.

JIMMY PACK · PHILADELPHIA, PA

Aleutian Islands Vigil

Daughter finds photos of World War II tribute to fallen soldiers.

My father, George DeMedeiros, was inducted into the Marine Corps on Jan. 4, 1942, less than a month after the bombing of Pearl Harbor. For most of my life, Dad never spoke of his time in the service. That changed when he became ill. We spent many hours together, and the stories he shared about his military life affected me profoundly.

Dad told me about his assignment at a secret air base in Alaska's Aleutian Islands, where the Marines served alongside the Navy. The branches engaged in a friendly competition, Dad said, but they all lived by the code that no brother was left alone or left behind. Dad recalled that the toughest duty they had was caring for the remains of the fallen soldiers brought to the base.

After a memorial service in the chapel, a guard stood watch over the fallen as they waited to go to their final resting places. A military escort accompanied the coffins that were flown home to waiting families.

But some of those who died could not be identified and became part of the large group who were missing in action or presumed dead. These were taken to a graveyard on the island, where they were buried with full military honors. Dad said the men felt bad for the families that didn't know the fate of their loved ones.

After Dad died, I found a stack of 8-by-10-inch photos. Mom didn't know the meaning of the pictures, but I felt certain that they documented the memorial service and burial of the unidentified soldiers. I later found out that Dad's friend Mickey McGrath, the base photographer, took the photos.

Several years later I visited Arlington National Cemetery. The sea of white crosses and the changing of the guard at the Tomb of the Unknown Soldier reminded me of Dad's story. The silence of the memorial spoke of great loss, and I wondered how to thank the veterans and their families for their sacrifice.

ELAINE DEMEDEIROS BENDER · TULARE, CA

Service members pay final respects to their brothers in arms.

Al Lopez joined the Army right out of high school in 1944.

New Citizen Soldier

Military service is a fast track to a change in national status.

Antelmo Lopez, my father, came to the U.S. from Mexico when he was a child, and graduated from high school in Los Angeles in June 1944. The family celebrated with a party, and then Al, as he was called, went straight to boot camp at Fort Bliss in El Paso, Texas, where he got a fresh haircut and a new uniform.

All was confusion at the time as a diverse group of young men from around the country began the process of forming a cohesive fighting unit. One morning at the crack of dawn, the sergeant came into the barracks. "Listen up!" he barked. "Garcia, Sanchez, Lopez, Hernandez, Rodriguez! Get up and be on the bus in 10 minutes."

With no idea of where they were headed, Dad and the others jumped out of bed, showered, put on uniforms and raced for the bus. At the courthouse, Dad found himself in front of a judge, who asked, "Who's the president of the United States?"

"Roosevelt," Dad said. The four other guys gave the same answer. The judge banged his gavel and said, "Congratulations. You're now all United States citizens."

Soon, Dad was on a massive troop ship headed to the Philippines. Despite disliking rules and regulations, Dad thrived in the Army, and by the time he came home from the service, he was a sergeant.

He married his high school sweetheart, my mother, Tillie, on April 19, 1947. The newlyweds moved into a small house on Soto Street in East Los Angeles.

After seeing an ad for trades that were open to veterans, Dad took advantage of the GI Bill and enrolled in an upholstery program. A true craftsman, Dad had a real knack for it, and after he completed the course, he started Garfield Upholstery. The shop became a fixture in the neighborhood, and was in business for 44 years.

DAVE LOPEZ · LONG BEACH, CA

Donald is seen here with singer-actress Lynn Kellogg in Vietnam in 1967.

Troupers for the Troops

A salute to USO entertainers in Vietnam.

The base camp of the 11th Armored Cavalry Regiment at Xuan Loc, South Vietnam, was knee-deep in mud in March 1967. About five months prior, we had left Long Binh to establish a new base camp in the jungle next to a large rubber plantation.

I was the medical platoon leader in 1st Squadron. My tentmate, Capt. Charles E. Vanetti, was a doctor and my boss. Our two-person tent had a wood pallet floor—an extreme luxury—and was complete with sandbags and a foxhole beside my cot that we could roll into when needed. Each night, we were serenaded to sleep by the sweet sounds of 155 mm howitzers firing over our heads from about 75 meters.

One gloomy, rainy evening we were keeping our spirits up at a tent we called the officers' club. My good friend 1st Lt. Ron Adams, our executive officer, asked me if I would be interested in a special mission: taking two Huey helicopters down to Saigon to pick up Jonathan Winters, who was coming to do a show for us.

I can't repeat what I said, but in proper English it was, "Are you kidding me?"

Several days later I flew to Saigon. Winters was touring with several actresses, including Lynn Kellogg and Frances Bergen. Wow! Those USO entertainers really put up with a lot for us: Winters had acrophobia, and he sat next to me by the open door of the chopper, pale and moaning. He was a real trouper.

I spent the day with him and, as expected, he entertained us with hilarious stories. He was impressed that I remembered one of his bits, "The Turtle Crossing the Pennsylvania Turnpike."

I had married my beautiful bride, Julie, five weeks before our unit got on the first of three ships to come to South Vietnam. My day with Jonathan Winters helped me remember life in the real world. I will always remember and respect what those performers went through to entertain the troops.

DONALD PRICE · TIGER, GA

Men Overboard!

Young deckhands think their day can't get any tougher.

In 1947, I was a 16-year-old deckhand aboard a merchant ship delivering medical supplies for the Army. The ship was anchored off the shore of Okinawa, Japan, and my shipmate Zach and I had the never-ending tasks of removing rust from the hull with a special sharp chipping hammer, then applying a lead paint sealer over the exposed area. We perched on a 12-foot-long wooden plank that hung outside the ship about 50 feet above the briny sea. Pulleys on each end of the plank allowed us to raise or lower our rig as needed.

It was near sunset, and we were hungry and tired from our labor and the pungent smell of the red paint. Over the *rat-a-tat* of our chipping hammers hitting the steel hull, we made out our first mate officer's announcement over the PA system: "All hands on deck! Prepare for securing the anchor and getting underway!"

We heard the wrenching and clanking of the anchor being pulled up, and saw the water under us begin to churn as the huge propeller started to swing the vessel toward open sea. The ship's foghorn gave a moaning farewell blast.

Anxious to get back on deck, we hurried to lift our rig, pulling the ropes on each end in unison. Then disaster struck.

Zach's rope slipped out of his hands, and his end of the plank fell, dropping us both into the dark waters of the Pacific Ocean. We surfaced, terrified and gasping for breath. Overhead, our bosun's mate was screaming: "Men overboard! Men overboard!"

Choking on seawater, we saw our lifeline, the Jacob's ladder, falling toward us and reaching the water's surface. Desperately tired, weak and shivering from the cold, we struggled mightily, pulling ourselves up the ladder. We gratefully accepted the extended hands of our shipmates, who reached down to help us make that final step onto the main deck.

The warm blankets and cups of hot black coffee they gave us were a godsend.

RAY RICHMOND · CYPRESS, CA

In 1947, Ray, right, was a 16-year-old seaman aboard a ship off the coast of Japan.

GI and War Chief

Scout wears sacred eagle feather for protection.

Crow tradition lays out four requirements to become a war chief: lead a successful war party into enemy territory, steal an adversary's weapon, touch an opponent without killing him and steal an enemy's horse.

Joseph Medicine Crow—who wore war paint under his uniform and kept a yellow eagle feather inside his helmet for protection while he served as a scout in the Army's 103rd Infantry Division during World War II—became the last of the Plains Indians to meet those requirements.

Medicine Crow was born in 1913 on the Crow Indian reservation near Lodge Grass, Montana. Given the name Winter Man in the hope that he would be able to withstand adversity, he was trained by his Grandfather Yellowtail to be a warrior. He grew up listening to stories of battles, including the conflict at Little Bighorn.

The first member of his tribe to attend college, Medicine Crow was working on an advanced degree in anthropology when the U.S. entered the war. In 1943, he enlisted.

On his return home, Medicine Crow followed the tradition of recounting his war deeds to the elders of his tribe. He told them about an operation at the Siegfried Line, in which he led a squad that blasted a hole in German defenses. He described colliding with a German soldier and knocking the man's rifle out of his hands. Locked in physical combat with the soldier, Medicine Crow overpowered the German, who cried out, and Medicine Crow released him.

When Medicine Crow described one final act as a scout—slipping onto the back of a German soldier's horse to stampede another 50—the elders reminded him that

LEFT: JOHN VAN HASSELT/CORBIS VIA GETTY IMAGES

he'd completed the four deeds needed to become a war chief.

Medicine Crow received the Bronze Star for meritorious service in 2008. He died in 2016 at 102.

NATALIE WYSONG

Medicine Crow was a war chief of the Crow Tribe in Montana.

A Tradition of Service

My father, Robert, was a chief reservist in the Coast Guard during World War II. Two weeks after I graduated from high school in 1950, the Korean War began and I joined the Navy. I served on six ships and several shore stations, retiring after 21 years. Here I am receiving my Good Conduct award from the commanding officer of the USS *Norfolk* in 1955.

ROGER RAE · HARRISONBURG, VA

CHAPTER 7

MOTORING MEMORIES

Fancy, fast or just practical, cars take
us along the road of life and its
many twists and turns.

Surf and Turf

Fans take in the action at the Daytona Beach and Road
Course on Feb. 26, 1956. Junior Johnson in No. 55, center,
later spun out and barrel rolled his Pontiac on the beach
section of the course. He wasn't injured.

Munda Maid Hits the Runway

Makeshift model satisfies technicians' driving needs.

My father, Floyd Westlake, joined the Army Air Forces in 1942 and was assigned to the 13th, known as the Jungle Air Force for its operations in the tropical islands in the Pacific theater. Following basic training, Dad shipped out to the Solomon Islands. He spent most of his time at the Munda Air Base in New Georgia.

Dad worked in the repair shop on base, fixing up planes damaged by heavy fighting. He and the other workers often had to make trips to the "bone yard" to salvage usable replacement parts and material. Since the base at Munda was quite large and very busy, it didn't have enough jeeps to go around—Dad sometimes had to wait for hours to get a jeep for one of these trips.

Dad and two of his buddies, Charles Orskog and a soldier I only ever knew as Slate, dealt with the jeep shortage by building their own. Each guy had a different skill: Dad was a welder, Orskog was a mechanic and Slate built hot rods.

They put together their vehicle using an engine from an old jeep, wheels from a bomb trailer and whatever they could find to build the chassis and the rest of the body. Slate rigged up the machine to drive like a race car down the runway. They named their creation the Munda Maid.

The group adopted a couple of other pals they found on the base—two stray dogs they named Susie and Wrinkles. When Dad, Slate and Orskog left the air base, they sold the Munda Maid to another soldier for $25. They also found homes for Susie and Wrinkles.

BRUCE WESTLAKE · KINNEAR, WY

Slate leans on the Munda Maid as Charles Orskog, sitting, and Floyd Westlake hold Susie and Wrinkles.

Ed proudly took ownership of the old mail truck in October 1950.

Mail Truck Stays in Circulation

Model A gets new life as a taxi.

Like many high school seniors in the 1950s, I dreamed of owning some kind of car. I worked in the shipping department of a bicycle parts distributor, and every afternoon I drove the company pickup to the post office to drop off the day's shipments.

On one of those trips, I saw a notice in the back room that the old mail truck was for sale. Like everyone in town, I knew it well. The 1931 Model A Ford had putted around our streets for about 20 years.

The post office was taking sealed bids for the truck, and I asked how and what to bid. I got a tip that someone bid $50, so I put in a bid for $60.50.

Waiting to hear whether I was the winner was the longest three months of my life. When I finally found out I was the happy owner of the truck, Dad made me buy liability insurance before I could even start the engine. I also had to buy two new rear tires. To my surprise, my girlfriend's parents allowed her to ride in the truck.

When I needed some gas money, I offered kids rides home from school for 5 cents each; 15 fares provided gas money for a week.

After graduation I sold the truck for $150. My dad just knew I had a bright future in automotive sales.

Around town these days, I still meet people who recognize me. They don't know my name, but they remember that I was the guy who owned the mail truck.

I have always felt very lucky that instead of only 15 minutes of fame, my moment lasted my entire senior year of high school. Buying the old mail truck was the best $60.50 I ever spent.

ED HAYNES · FORT SMITH, AR

The 1931 Ford had putted around our streets for about 20 years.

Umpteen tries later, John mastered parallel parking with the Bug.

Parking Lessons

Mom takes the first shift.

———

Practice, practice, practice. That's what I needed to pass the Ohio driver's license exam in 1974. And the best place to do that was behind Logan Elm High School in Circleville when nobody was around.

I had my learner's permit. Dad had insisted that it was important to learn to drive a manual transmission, so I was already pretty smooth with our family's Volkswagen Bug. But parallel parking was my nemesis.

One Sunday afternoon, with my mother in the passenger seat, I drove the Bug around to the back of the school. Mom exited the car to watch and give encouragement. I got the car into position near the sets of posts that marked the practice parking spot. The posts were set in concrete in metal cans, and I pulled carefully ahead of the front two. I put the Bug in reverse and with my right hand resting on the back of the passenger seat as I'd been taught, inched the car backward, waiting until just the right moment to crank the steering wheel.

Ka-thump!

"Oh, John!" Mom yelled. I'd backed into one of the posts. If I'd been wedging between parked cars, I would have dented one.

"Don't worry," Mom said. "It just takes practice. Try again."

So I did try, again and again, each time with different turns and cuts, but always got the same result. After one more attempt, I got out of the car, walked back to a downed post and returned it to its upright position. I got back in the car and buckled my seat belt. Mom leaned in the passenger window.

"John, maybe we should call it a day. You can come back next Sunday, with your father."

Four weeks later, thanks to all that practice, practice, practice I did, I managed to ace the parallel parking portion of the Ohio driver's license exam.

JOHN SCANLAN · HILTON HEAD ISLAND, SC

Drive like My Brother

Advice points him in the direction of the Park Avenue.

———

My older brother Alfred told me, "If you ever drive a Park Avenue Buick, you will never want another car."

In the late 1990s, he owned a dark blue 1989 model. He called me to say he was ready to buy a new car, and was willing to give me a good deal on the one he was replacing. Alfred always maintained his cars in perfect condition inside and out, and this one was no exception.

I felt like a king as I drove that Buick home. After driving it for a year, I liked it so much that I began looking for a second one for my wife. In 2000, we saw another blue beauty in a parking lot. Its owner wasn't around, so we left a note on its windshield: "If you ever want to sell your car, please call this number."

Several months later, a woman called me. She told me she had only ever driven her car to church and the beauty shop. This proverbial "little old lady car" had a mere 42,000 miles on it.

We continued to be impressed by these cars, and in the fall of 2001, we found yet another one. We bought our third dark blue 1989 Buick Park Avenue, giving us a three-peat on this model that, unfortunately, was discontinued in 2005.

Each of those cars got over 200,000 miles. I'm happy to say that my brother was right—for me, there's no better ride than a Buick Park Avenue.

STAN VOUDRIE · MORTON, IL

Park Avenue was a luxury selection from GM's Buick division.

Winter Tires Give Snow the Slip

Thank Finland for creating the first models in the 1930s.

A 1960s Chicago radio DJ used to call snow "freezy skid stuff." The joking reference to hair tonic was cold comfort to motorists on slippery roads, but a few had a partial remedy: snow tires.

Finland introduced winter tires in 1934. The Kelirengas truck tire tamed dirt roads slick with ice and snow. In North America, Firestone's Town & Country and Goodyear's Suburbanite arrived in 1952. On rear-drive wheels, the tires improved acceleration and stability but did little for steering and braking.

The all-season tires of the 1970s seemed to make snow tires obsolete, but new tire technology in recent decades has spawned a revival.

The popularity of rally motor sports in Europe provided a convenient testing ground for tires such as the Hakkapeliitta from Nokian, which helped to cement the reputation of Finnish rally drivers in the 1950s and '60s. The tires used hardened studs to improve traction on slick mountain roads.

Studded tires became available from many manufacturers for consumer use by the mid-1960s; however, road damage prompted many North American cities and towns to ban them. Tiremakers opted for less aggressive rubber adjuncts, such as carborundum and even walnut shells.

Silica compounds brought great improvements to tire traction in colder weather, and nearly all major brands use them in winter tires and even all-season tires. Bridgestone uses a multicell rubber compound in its Blizzak tires that enhances grip on ice.

Winter-capable tires are identified by the pictogram of the three-peaked mountain snowflake embossed on the sidewall of every qualifying tire sold in North America. The U.S. Tire Manufacturers Association and the Tire and Rubber Association of Canada created the standard.

Two Canadian provinces, Quebec and British Columbia, require drivers by law to use winter tires each snow season.

RUSS MAKI

Snow tires saved many winter riders from the tyranny of chains.

Ford's V-8 was big in hot rods, as in this Model A. Don Francisco, an automotive writer, looks it over in 1956.

Wow, Everybody Can Have a V-8

Ford's flathead design powers millions of cars over 21-year production history.

Check under the hood of one of today's vehicles and you're likely to see a turbo-charged, direct-injected four- or six-cylinder engine. But 90 years ago, America fell for a different engine, and the love affair lasted decades.

In 1932, Henry Ford unveiled the first mass-market V-8, a motor previously available only in pricier cars. Ford's simpler flathead design was cheaper to make. From 1932 to 1953 it built 25 million, ranking Ford's V-8 among the 20th century's most important automotive engines.

The mass-market V-8 concept is credited as Henry Ford's last engineering contribution to the company.

In 1934, Henry Ford received a letter that was purportedly from bank robber Clyde Barrow of the infamous crime duo Bonnie and Clyde. The letter praises the flathead V-8 for its ability to outrun pursuers. "While I still have got breath in my lungs," the author writes, "I will tell you what a dandy car you make. I have drove Fords exclusively when I could get away with one."

Criminals weren't the only ones impressed with the flathead's performance. As early as the late 1930s, aftermarket modifiers such as Edelbrock, Thickstun and Offenhauser worked on developing performance parts to increase the V-8's output, making the flathead the first popular hot-rod engine.

Ford introduced a smaller version of the engine for its European market. It debuted in North America in 1937 as the V8-60 for its peak output of 60 horsepower. Acceleration was significantly weaker than the bigger V-8, and slow sales ended its North American distribution after 1940. But the engine was in production in Europe into the 1960s. The V8-60 also gained popularity in modified form on the midget car racing circuit.

The Beach Boys, associated as much with California car culture as surfing, paid homage to the flathead V-8 in their 1963 album *Little Deuce Coupe*. The title track peaked at No. 4 on the Billboard chart the next year.

RUSS MAKI

Intermittent Success

Brilliance of wiper patent awarded 55 years ago clouded by decades of lawsuits.

An errant champagne cork that hit engineer Robert Kearns in the eye on his wedding night did more than disrupt the evening; it inspired him to design the mechanism for intermittent windshield wipers.

Kearns, a loyal Ford Motor Co. customer, approached the company with a proposal that he manufacture the system for Ford cars. While impressed, Ford didn't agree and instead appropriated the design. Kearns waged a decades-long legal war against automakers around the world. In the end, he won millions in settlements, but not before his fight cost him his career, his marriage and a stint in a psychiatric hospital.

Kearns' eye injury caused him to consider the act of blinking, which adjusts to environmental conditions. Windshield wipers that worked the same way, he reasoned, could improve visibility during driving. Fourteen years after the fateful night of the cork, in 1967, Kearns got the first of some 30 patents he ultimately acquired on his wiper design.

He first showed a prototype of his invention, installed on his 1962 Galaxie, to Ford in 1963.

Kearns thought an agreement was imminent, but Ford remained noncommittal for years. In the meantime, the automaker built an intermittent system of its own, using design details Kearns had provided. The system became available on Ford cars in 1969.

In 1976, Kearns' son bought a Mercedes-Benz intermittent wiper system. After Kearns realized it was based on his design, he broke down. Then he became obsessed with forcing the industry to acknowledge the invention was his. He sued Ford for patent infringement in 1978.

His wife divorced him in 1989. Ford eventually offered him a settlement, but Kearns refused. A federal jury later awarded him $10.2 million. In 1992, he won a case against Chrysler for millions more. But his dream of being the manufacturer of the device never materialized. Kearns died in 2005. In 2008, Greg Kinnear played him in the movie *Flash of Genius*.

RUSS MAKI

Robert Kearns took on the auto industry in an epic legal battle.

A Daring Attempt at Rescue

Avanti moves forward with racy styling as Studebaker stumbles.

A rguably the automotive design leader after World War II, Studebaker failed to thrive despite its innovations. By the early '60s, operations were in a tailspin. But the maker that began in the 1850s as wagon builders had one final hurrah.

The Avanti broke the styling mold for sport coupes. The long hood, short rear deck and hiplike bulge made for a seductive look that survives today on Ford's Mustang, Chevrolet's Camaro and others.

Studebaker unveiled the fiberglass-bodied Avanti in 1962, but production problems delayed delivery and the company's precarious condition scared off many prospective buyers. Only 3,834 Avantis sold in 1963 and 809 in 1964, after the South Bend, Indiana, factory ceased production. Taken over by independent coachbuilders, however, the hand-built milestone car outlived the Studebaker marque by four decades.

Designer Raymond Loewy, who oversaw many of Studebaker's head-turning creations, got the assignment in 1961 to create a "halo" model that would bring customers back into dealership showrooms. Loewy had a prototype ready for the 1962 New York Auto Show.

The design team based the car on the company's compact Lark, a strategy Ford later used with its Falcon platform in developing the Mustang.

Studebaker stuffed a 289-cubic-inch engine under the hood with optional supercharger that turned out 290 horsepower. At Bonneville, the supercharged car set 29 speed records for production cars, nearly reaching 170 mph in the flying mile.

Studebaker continued to slide, and its Avanti production ended in late 1963. Two Studebaker dealers, Nathan Altman and Leo Newman, came to Avanti's rescue however with a plan to build the car independently.

With the powerful Studebaker V-8 and other running gear no longer available, the company used Chevrolet components and made subtle body adaptations. Altman and Newman hand built Avanti IIs in small numbers into the early 1980s, when they sold the business. New owner Stephen Blake updated the design and offered a first-ever convertible version. But warranty coverage of paint problems sent the company into bankruptcy in 1986.

But the story didn't end there. The post-bankruptcy New Avanti Motor Corp. began building cars using a chassis platform obtained from General Motors. A series of owners followed, maintaining intermittent production on GM and Ford platforms until 2006.

RUSS MAKI

AUTOMOTIVE MOTIVATION

How do you make engine parts appealing?

« 1949

Tell a Reliable Story

The Electric Storage Battery Co. in Philadelphia was a leading supplier from the earliest days of motoring; postwar car owners would have been familiar with the striking look of an Exide, with its graphic black and red styling. Its ad evokes a strong theme of the era that cast men as driven breadwinners who keep the economy rolling.

1962 »

Spark Interest

In 1962, when all thoughts were on the promise of space after John Glenn's orbit of Earth that February, AC Spark Plug positions itself as a future-facing company with a clever ad that makes its ordinary car part look like a rocket.

1952 **Fuel the Imagination**

Ukrainian-born Boris Artzybasheff, who immigrated to the United States in 1919, was a prolific commercial artist and illustrator. He drew some 200 covers for *Time*, created ad campaigns for dozens of clients and worked on acclaimed children's books before his death in 1965. Artzybasheff had a fondness for machines, and liked to draw them with human characteristics such as hands and faces. His many ads for Shell motor oil in the early '50s, featuring the mildly terrifying acid demon wreaking havoc on innocent engines, show his creative mind at its most astonishing and effective.

ALL PUMPED UP

Drivers converge on a service station in New York City for their gas rations during World War II. Similar scenes would play out at the pumps during the energy crisis in the 1970s.

Dad's Upscale Clunker

A sleek Series 61 sedan turns the family into Cadillac people.

Dad never owned a new car. Money was tight in our family, but my father was a master mechanic who could keep old clunkers running. In early 1953, he shocked my mother, my brother Jack and me by bringing home a 1941 Cadillac Series 61 four-door sedan. Mother was not pleased, saying we couldn't afford it.

"We aren't Cadillac people," she said.

Jack and I thought it was one of the most beautiful cars we'd ever seen. It was dark metallic green with the torpedo body style, whitewall tires and acres of glittering chrome.

After a couple of Sunday drives, my mother changed her mind. She said the ride felt like "floating on a cloud."

Jack was two years older than me and already had his driver's license. He started driving the car immediately. I could hardly wait the six months before I could get my license. Fortunately, Hagerstown had many lonely back roads where you could take a turn behind the wheel with no one around to question your age.

That Cadillac took the family on a memorable road trip to Canada, which was our first time out of the United States. Not long after that trip, Dad bought a 1940 Dodge coupe and turned the Caddy over to Jack and me. All we had to do was pay for insurance, registration, tires, gas and anything else the car needed. Those expenses ate up most of our limited income. But no matter—we had wheels!

Jack commuted to college during the week, so I used the car on nights and weekends. At the close of my sophomore year, a friend volunteered me to run the coat check at the junior/senior prom with Carolyn, a pretty and smart girl from our biology class. Carolyn lived in the country, so I had to pick her up. Dressed in a pale blue prom dress, she looked beautiful. The next day we went to the class picnic some distance away. With my attention on more pleasant matters, I failed to notice the fuel gauge. That big V-8 engine had drained the tank. Luckily we made it home.

The Caddy took us on many more dates. On one of them, I gave Carolyn an engagement ring. We were 80 miles and six mountains apart during our first year of college, and the Cadillac made the trip flawlessly many times.

I still think fondly of that big green Caddy and the wonderful memories it gave us.

DALE SEBURN · HAGERSTOWN, MD

This is the '48 Sixty Special. Tail fins first appeared on Cadillacs in the 1948 model year.

LUXURY ON WHEELS

Created by an automotive pioneer with a penchant for efficiency and precision, the Cadillac set a high standard from the start.

1902: Henry Martyn Leland, engineer and inventor, recasts the failing Detroit Motor Co. to build luxury cars.

1903: Naming his company after the founder of Detroit, Antoine de la Mothe Cadillac, Leland rolls out his Model A, left. By 1908, he has five models. All use parts that are interchangeable—a key to efficient manufacturing that Leland learned working in the gunsmithing industry before the Civil War.

1909: William Durant of General Motors buys Cadillac. Now in his mid-60s, Leland stays on to run production. Six years later, Cadillac builds the first production car with a V-8 engine.

1930: Cadillac comes out with the first V-16-engine production cars, including the stylish 452 Fleetwood roadster, right. The engines produce 160 horsepower and, with luck, can reach speeds of 100 mph, a technical milestone at the time.

1948: Cadillac's Sixty Special is the first car with tail fins, opposite page. Late the following year, the 1 millionth Cadillac rolls off the production line.

1950s: In an era of automotive innovation, Cadillac in 1954 is the first carmaker to make power steering standard on all models. In 1959, the Eldorado takes tail fins to sublime heights, left.

1965: Caddies are equipped with tilting and telescoping steering wheels. Two years later, the Fleetwood Eldorado is the first Cadillac with front-wheel drive.

1970: The Eldorado has the largest mass-produced engine in history—8.2 liters with 400 horsepower. Two years later, safety belts are standard in all Cadillac models.

OPEN-AIR DRIVING IN A FANCY CARRIAGE

A cousin of mine, Bob, had a 1903 Cadillac with wood body, padded seats, chain drive and a one-cylinder engine. It also had carbide lights, but as far as I was concerned, it was strictly a daytime, fair-weather mode of transportation. Naturally, it was a crank start, which was my job. Most of the time it even started. Two mysteries I never solved as an 8-year-old were how that Caddy stopped and how it backed up. It could do both. I'll give that old Cadillac one thing: It got a lot of smiles per mile.
STEVEN RUEDY
NORMAN, OK

A DOLLAR BILL AND SOME BONDO SEAL THE DEAL

In 1974, when we were about 19, my buddy Jim Neforos and I bought a 1962 Cadillac from a guy named— no kidding—Joe Cadillac for $125. It was black, with four doors and two sets of fins. It needed some work, and we weren't exactly car guys, but we thought it would be fun. We wrote "Cadillac" on a dollar bill and ripped it in half. That was our contract.

My grandfather, a carpenter, helped us repair the fenders with two-by-fours and a lot of Bondo. My grandmother sewed red curtains with black tassels for the interior. (I have no idea what we were thinking there.)

We kept it for a year or two before selling it for $425. We each still have our half-dollar today.
JOE ARNOLD · BOLIVAR, MO

MAGNIFICENT MILER

DAD PROMISED THAT IF I KEPT MY GRADES UP, HE'D buy me a car. And he kept his word. In my senior year of high school, I became the proud owner of a white 1963 Cadillac convertible.

The car was almost as old as me, but that's what made it special. My Cadillac had a 390 V-8 engine, with power seats, power windows, red leather upholstery and, best of all, tail fins. What more could a car-crazy teenager ask for?

My Caddy had some rust, so when I went away to college, I jumped at the chance to buy rust-free doors and fenders at a Florida junkyard. I had to store them in my dorm room until my buddy Boo could install them. Fortunately, my roommate Rob was also a classic car buff and never complained about having to navigate the maze of spare parts.

By late summer 1979, the Cadillac had a fresh paint job. My brother and I drove it to Florida. We listened to tapes most of the trip, until a mysterious lack of traffic on I-95 in South Carolina made us curious enough to turn on the radio.

News flash: Hurricane! With motels full, we had no choice but to sleep in the Cadillac. The 4,500-pound car rocked back and forth all night, and the rain was so fierce the doors filled with water. By morning, however, the storm had passed—and the Caddy had kept us safe.

I nicknamed my Cadillac the Emperor—and, indeed, to me it was the king of the road. Today, my 1963 Cadillac showroom wall sign honors that fin-tastic first car.

LUKE MILLER · URBANDALE, IA

Luke relaxes after finishing another wax job on the Emperor.

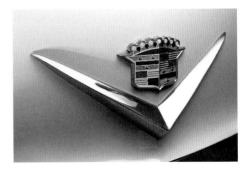

CUPID MAKES A PERFECT MATCH

It was just Mom and me when I was a girl. One Saturday, we heard a scream from across the alley, and saw a man working on a big black Cadillac clutching his arm. The engine had caught fire and burned him.

Mom dressed his wound with iodine and bandages, and he asked her out as a thank-you.

Long story short: That man became my stepdad—the best in the world. I even got two brothers out of the deal.

We called that car the Cupid Cadillac. It was the best thing that ever happened to Mom and me.

RUTH COCKERHAM · WAUKEGAN, IL

SOME EXTRAS ARE NECESSITIES

In 1955, my father wanted a Cadillac but couldn't afford anything except a stripped-down entry-level model, a Series 62 coupe. He told the salesman at the dealership that he didn't even want a radio installed, which was an extra charge at the time.

"We'll throw the radio in for free," the salesman said. "No Caddy is leaving here without a radio."

MARVIN J. OWEN · SIERRA VISTA, AZ

IF YOU CAN DREAM IT, YOU CAN BUY IT

AT MY HIGH SCHOOL IN 1963, MAYBE A
dozen kids owned cars and drove them to classes each day. I was one of them. I had a 1947 Ford Super Deluxe sedan. I was lucky enough to have a steady job at a hardware store after school and on Saturdays making $1.25 an hour, which was good money.

I delivered the newspaper to one of our customers who worked at the hospital. On the way, I'd stop to admire a cool 1956 Cadillac Coupe DeVille hardtop in the parking lot. I tried to imagine what it would be like to drive it, never dreaming that I would ever get the chance.

I knew who owned it, and one day she came into the store. As I waited on her, I mentioned her good-looking car. She told me that she had ordered a new car and was trading in the Caddy. But she was willing to sell it for what the dealership was paying on the trade-in—$500.

I did some quick figuring. I was real interested, I told her.

Dad and I went to the bank—the car was going to be mine. But the deal got even sweeter. The seller decided to buy my 1947 Ford for her son. That meant I had to borrow only $425.

Dwight bought this snazzy rose Caddy on his part-time salary as a store clerk.

It would be impossible today to get a 7-year-old Cadillac for $500, or even $15,000.

I had some wonderful times in that car. When my grandpa saw the motor, he said, "Looks like you'll pass anything but a gas station."

He wasn't far off. Darn sure wish I still had it.

DWIGHT CAMPBELL · ATLANTA, MI

The Cochrans enjoyed the Cadillac life for a year, courtesy of Pat's mom, shown, left, with Joanne and young Julie.

IN THE LAP OF LUXURY, IT'S BEST TO KEEP YOUR DISTANCE

My wife, Joanne, and I were overseas missionaries in the 1970s. During our furlough year in the United States, we needed a vehicle, so my mother loaned us her 1969 Cadillac Coupe DeVille.

I was embarrassed to be driving a Cadillac as a church-supported missionary. When we toured congregations to talk about our work, I'd park far away from the church so no one would see it.

PAT COCHRAN · DALLAS, TX

Go Big or Go Home

Land Yacht is family's guide through Airstream country.

My father owned a successful business in New Jersey, but as he aged, the sinus condition he suffered from all his life worsened. His doctor advised him to relocate to a warmer climate. My parents didn't want to quit living in New Jersey entirely. Instead, they bought a 33-foot trailer. That fall of 1952 was the start of our annual trips to Florida to spend the winter at Briny Breezes, a trailer park on the ocean between Lake Worth and Delray Beach. Today, Briny Breezes is one of just two mobile home parks in Florida that incorporated as towns.

At the time, my brothers and I didn't think about how unique it was to leave New Jersey schools in November and attend Florida schools through March every year. It drove the teachers in both states crazy.

After two years of towing the 7,000-pound Palace Ranchome back and forth each season, Dad had had enough. He stored it in Florida and had it installed at our site each fall.

Meanwhile, my parents looked for a smaller trailer for summer trips around New Jersey. Dad suggested an Airstream, but Mom said no.

"Those are the ugliest trailers I've ever seen!"

Two more trailers later, Mom changed her mind about owning an Airstream. It helped that the first one they bought was a brand-new 1959 Land Yacht—a luxury model.

My parents joined the Wally Byam Caravan Club and, like other club members, affixed their identification number, 1975, to the front and rear of their Airstream.

Soon, they were traveling to club caravans across the country, including the Second International Rally at Wisconsin Dells in 1959. The rally leader, known as the wagonmaster, coordinated all arriving members, who parked their trailers in a wagon-wheel formation.

Each caravan lasted three or four days and put on planned events for adults and children. The main event usually featured a well-known musician or TV personality. Members often exchanged their money for $2 bills, which they used at local stores to alert merchants that they were with the traveling Airstream club.

Members treated each other like family. When you spotted other members on the road, you could look up their IDs in the directory for name, hometown, number of children and whether they could put up a fellow member for an evening.

Airstream membership paid off in other ways over the years. In 1973, for example, I was a salesman for a New Jersey Chevrolet-Oldsmobile

Airstream Inc. was founded in 1931 by Wally Byam in Jackson Center, Ohio. Each aluminum-sided trailer has an average of 3,000 rivets.

dealership when, one late-winter night, a couple came in asking for me. The man said they'd seen my parents three days before.

"I think you have me confused with someone else," I told him. "My parents are on an Airstream caravan in Mexico, on their way to Panama."

But the man confirmed that it was the same couple. He said his new car had had an electrical short that caused it to catch fire. Within about 25 minutes, both car and trailer were destroyed.

"Your parents gave us clothes and a bed for the night in their Airstream," he said.

The next day, my parents drove the stranded couple to the airport in Mexico City, bought them their tickets for New Jersey and gave them cash for incidentals.

Before seeing them off, my father suggested to the couple that if they were thinking of buying a GM car when they got home, they should look me up because I knew all the extras needed for pulling a trailer.

Of course, that was one of the easiest sales of an Oldsmobile 98 I ever made.

My parents owned nine Airstreams over the years: seven trailers, a 31-foot RV and one built on a Ford Econoline chassis.

My younger brother keeps the family tradition alive, traveling across the Southeast with a 31-foot Airstream.

KEITH GALLAWAY · PORT MURRAY, NJ

Rolling in Silver

Life is full of surprises when you grow up in an Airstream.

My parents wanted a different kind of life. In 1959, they sold their home in Chicago and bought a new 28-foot Airstream to travel and live on the road full time. When our adventure began, I was 18 months old. For the next few years, that Airstream was the only home I knew.

My father became a traveling salesman, and we went all through the West. I had birthdays in Idaho and Christmases in Arizona. An only child, I learned to entertain myself. This nomadic existence continued until I was 6, when my parents decided to settle down so that I could attend school.

Having grown up with frigid winters, my parents chose to live in Orange County, California. They were devoted travelers by this point. Each June, the day after school was out, we packed up the

Safari models, with more contemporary design inside and out, were popular in the 1960s, far left. Airstream interiors are famously luxe, with kitchens rivaling those at home, whether in the '60s, top left, or in a 2019 Classic model, bottom left.

The Airstream slept four, but when my grandparents joined us, I slept in a hammock Dad rigged up for me over the kitchen counter.

Airstream and hit the road, never returning until the day before school started in the fall. This was the pattern for the next 11 years—I didn't spend a summer in California until after I graduated.

The Airstream slept four, but when my grandparents joined us, I slept in a hammock Dad rigged up for me over the kitchen counter.

He was quite resourceful when it came to using every nook and cranny for storage. It wasn't until years later, when I lived in my own RV for a year, that I realized the many choices you have to make as a full-time traveler. You buy only what you can consume; trailers have no space for any extra clothes or nonessentials. If you add one thing, something else must go.

I gained a love of travel but there were a few times my father thought I wasn't appreciating

this opportunity to the fullest. If he saw me reading in the backseat, he would admonish me to look at the amazing country we were driving through.

After I no longer traveled with them, my parents went on longer and more distant trips. They used their Airstream together until my mother died. Then Dad took it on regular visits to Oregon until he was well into his 80s.

Although my husband and I love to travel with an RV, my parents' Airstream didn't suit our needs. We sold it to a buyer from South Korea, who had it shipped there by sea train.

Amazingly, the saga of our beloved 1959 Airstream continues on the other side of the world.

KIMBERLY BLACK · NAMPA, ID

Sand, Water, Gas and Combustion

What could possibly go wrong?

O ne Saturday morning in Los Angeles in 1941, during my second year in high school, my buddy Bob Thompson asked me to help fix his new 1930 DeSoto. He loved that car, which had a convertible top, wire wheels, a rumble seat and a chrome winged goddess hood ornament that served as a radiator cap.

Sand in his tank was clogging up the fuel line, so every few miles he had to stop, disconnect the gas line from the carburetor and blow through the line to clear the sand. Taking it to a repair shop was out, as he didn't want to spend money on anything but girls—and not a lot on them.

Bob drained the gas out of his tank and filled it with water, which, he explained, would slosh out the sand while he was driving.

"Slosh it out?" I asked.

"I'll fishtail the car with the tank drain unplugged. The water will slosh around in the tank and stir up the sand, and it'll drain out with the water."

Not being much of a car guy, that made perfect sense to me, but I had a question. "How will the car run if there's no gas?"

"That's where you come in." He explained that I would sit on the front fender with a can of gas, and pour it slowly into the carburetor while he swerved down the street. I felt a little proud that he'd picked me to help him with this reasonable plan.

I took my position by the beautiful winged goddess, gas can in hand, and located the target: a 2-inch hole in the top of the carburetor. It seemed pretty spacious enough.

Bob knelt and unscrewed the drain plug. Water trickled out, and he jumped in behind the wheel. "OK, pour a little gas in."

As I added gas, he stepped on the starter. The car started, then sputtered, and I poured in more. This was simple: I just had to keep a small stream of gas running continuously into the carburetor.

Friends Bob and Bill in 1942.

Bob put the car in gear, and it lurched, nearly throwing me off the fender. I grabbed what I could—a headlight—and managed to stay on. We picked up speed and Bob zigzagged down Alviso Avenue as I hung on for dear life. Gasoline splashed everywhere, and Bob yelled over the windshield, "Don't get any gas on the exhaust manifold—it could catch fire." Swell. Now I had to avoid incineration.

We made it around the block and Bob stopped to have a look in the tank. "Uh-oh," he said. "Water's still running out. We'll have to go around again."

I didn't know the phrase "No way, Jose," or that would have been my response. I got back on the fender and we were off on another version of Mr. Toad's Wild Ride.

This time the tank emptied. Bob put some gas in, and we took the old DeSoto for a spin. After a couple of miles, Bob had to stop. He opened the hood and blew as hard as he could into the gas line.

BILL LIVINGSTONE · GOLETA, CA

See and Do

At 3 years old in 1935, I watch as my grandfather pumps up
a tire. I went on to a career as an auto technician and teacher.
My sons and great-grandsons followed in my footsteps.

EDWARD REED · GROVELAND, MA

CHAPTER 8

....

SEEING STARS

They wow on the silver screen or on TV,
but up close in person, celebrities like
Fess Parker and John Gavin are
pretty friendly.

Fab Four

Carol Burnett, bottom, starred in her groundbreaking variety show
on CBS starting in 1967. *The Carol Burnett Show* won 25 Emmys
in its 11 years on TV, aided by the stellar comedy chops of
Tim Conway, Vicki Lawrence and Harvey Korman.

Trick of the Light Sitcom

Who could resist the enchantment of *Bewitched*?

Bewitched had many components of the typical TV family sitcom: suburban setting, stressed-out husband, sweet wife, nosy neighbors. But its unique premise—that ad executive Darrin Stephens married a witch and was desperate to keep it a secret—delivered comedy gold. The show was the No. 2 hit in the Nielsen ratings at the end of its first season in 1965.

Zany clashes each week between the magical and mortal worlds had *Bewitched* feeling more like a throwback to big-screen screwball farce than the polite humor of Ozzie and Harriet. Underneath was a sly poke at domestic bliss.

Darrin forbade Samantha from using her powers. The "mortal way" was the path of virtue, he claimed. Sam tried to comply, but always wound up using magic, usually to rescue Darrin, if not the world. If saving humanity interrupted her housekeeping, Sam would twitch her nose at the Hoover to make it clean by itself—to the envy of women everywhere.

Bewitched ended in 1972, but its influence lives on in the plotlines of *Harry Potter*, the groove of *Mad Men*—even, perhaps, in the technological wizardry of robotic vacuums.

MARY-LIZ SHAW

THE TWO DARRINS

Dick York's sudden departure as Darrin at the end of season five in 1969 was one of TV lore's most enduring mysteries. No one on- or off-set ever explained why Dick Sargent was suddenly playing Sam's husband. Fans speculated about it for years, with theories ranging from a simple contract dispute to the claim that York had fallen inconveniently in love with his co-star. The truth, as York told *FilmFax* magazine years later, was sadly worse: He had suffered a severe back injury during the filming of *They Came to Cordura* (1959) and became addicted to pain pills. York had to quit the show after fainting on the set.

REAL-LIFE TEAM

Elizabeth Montgomery and her third husband, William Asher, a veteran TV director for *I Love Lucy* and other hits, chose *Bewitched* to do together with Montgomery as star and Asher as director and later producer. Sol Saks wrote the pilot based on the movie *I Married a Witch* (1942) and *Bell, Book and Candle*, a play and later a 1958 movie. Saks never wrote another episode, but being the show's creator made him a millionaire.

....

MORE SWITCHES

Even before the infamous Darrin switcheroo, the cast of *Bewitched* sustained other changes. Alice Pearce played nosy neighbor Gladys Kravitz until 1966, when Pearce died of ovarian cancer. Her replacement, Sandra Gould, played Gladys as less likable and more meddlesome. Irene Vernon played Louise, wife of Darrin's boss, Larry Tate, for two seasons before Kasey Rogers replaced her.

....

ABOUT THAT TWITCH

Sam's signature move— the nose wriggle—was something Montgomery did naturally when she was nervous. It wasn't a wriggle exactly—more of a quick shift of the upper lip, which was enhanced by speeding up the film during editing.

MOTHER!

Agnes Moorehead was a veteran actor with 40 years of radio, stage and screen experience—including as a

trusted member of Orson Welles' Mercury Players— when she joined the cast as Sam's mother, Endora. Moorehead played the frightening mother-in-law with gusto. She was upset when York left the cast, reportedly declaring "I do not like the change" at Sargent's first rehearsal.

....

ROGUE'S GALLERY

Bewitched featured a vast cast of supporting players who, despite success on stage and screen, were best remembered for their brief pops on the show. These included Paul Lynde as Uncle Arthur, Bernard Fox as Dr. Bombay, Marion Lorne as lovable Aunt Clara, Alice Ghostley as Esmeralda and Maurice Evans as Sam's father, Maurice.

First-Flight Butterflies

Sitting by a movie star is a little too exciting.

The first time I flew was to visit my recently married sister in Oklahoma in 1956. I was 16, and I drove with my parents, Levio and Josephine Del Carlo, from our home in Sanger, California, to Los Angeles, where we boarded a huge airplane—at least I thought it was huge.

Mom and Dad sat across the aisle from me. The seat next to mine was empty, but there was a "reserved" sign on it. As I wondered whether my seatmate would be friendly, down the aisle came a tall, scruffy man who took the reserved spot. He was handsome, with longish hair, and was casually dressed in jeans. I was not sure that my rugged partner was going to be the nice, friendly conversation partner I'd hoped for on this trip. When he sat down and crossed his legs, I did notice that he had the biggest feet I'd ever seen!

The plane took off, and my heart pounded with excitement. Soon the man and I started chatting, and I found I was flying next to the actor Fess Parker, famous for playing Davy Crockett in the TV series and movies about the frontiersman. Mr. Parker couldn't have been nicer, and I introduced him to my parents, who weren't nearly as impressed as I was.

The flight was fairly short, but to my dismay and embarrassment, I began to feel nauseous. As the plane descended, I felt worse, and told Mr. Parker I was going to throw up. He grabbed an airsickness bag and held it for me as I gagged and spit up. The plane landed, but I didn't get to see my first landing because my head was in a bag.

I still felt queasy as we left the plane, and he kindly asked how I was. I thanked him for helping me and we said goodbye.

I have thought back many times to this story, one of several highlights in

Jean, center, was eager for glamorous adventure on the 1956 flight with her parents.

my life, and it still makes me smile. And I wonder sometimes if Mr. Parker ever told anyone about the time he held an airsickness bag for a teenager on her first airplane flight.

JEAN LANE · FRESNO, CA

Canadian-born Greene was a radio personality and actor, as well as a hit musician.

Ma'am, Let Me Offer You My Seat

Lorne Greene gives up his shotgun post.

My mother-in-law, Thelma, needed to see specialists at the Mayo Clinic in Rochester, Minnesota, in 1976. I went along as her caregiver, and brought my children, Kim, 3, and Eric, a baby. Thelma was frail and rode in a wheelchair through the Savannah airport. I must have looked a bit frantic because many people offered to help me.

There was a buzz of excitement as we waited to board, and I saw that the actor Lorne Greene was on our flight. *Bonanza* was a family TV favorite; Greene played Ben Cartwright, the handsome owner of the Ponderosa ranch. I felt certain we wouldn't see much of him, since I had a small brood to look after, and he would be in first class.

Once we were in the air, the flight attendant told me that when we reached Atlanta, I should deplane ahead of the other passengers, so we could catch our connecting flight. When we landed, one attendant helped Thelma with the wheelchair and a second took Kim. I carried Eric down to the tarmac, where an airport limousine (a station wagon, actually) waited to take us to our gate for the connecting flight.

Mr. Greene sat in the front passenger seat of the limo. He graciously helped Thelma, a gentle woman who never asked for special favors, into his spot, then he helped me and my kids into the backseat. He climbed into the rear of the vehicle and perched on our luggage.

I pretended to be nonchalant and did not ask for his autograph—which I regret! He told me he'd been in Savannah filming the TV miniseries *Roots*, and was on his way to attend a fundraiser for Hubert Humphrey, who was considering a presidential run.

At the end of our short ride, Mr. Greene helped Thelma out of the car and into the wheelchair as airport workers got us onto our flight. Lorne Greene was a true gentleman.

NELDA R. BISHOP · STATESBORO, GA

Joanne bonded with Mom Peggy, here in 1954, and later by laughing together at Lucille Ball's fresh takes.

More than a Housewife

Lucy's slapstick knocks down barriers.

M y mother, Peggy, and I watched *I Love Lucy* together. I sat cross-legged on the floor in front of our black-and-white TV while Mom stood behind me at the ironing board, pressing Dad's shirts.

The show's formula relied on Lucy's relentless determination to make her mark. Mom and I both understood that Lucy, as a housewife, believed she was meant to do more than what her husband, Ricky, and society defined for her. Once Lucy set her mind on an outcome, barriers were merely something to hop over, crawl under or ignore.

One of my favorite episodes clearly shows Lucy's ambition. Lucy meets a famous Italian director, who offers her an audition. She takes it upon herself to learn about the culture and visits a vineyard. There, she ends up barefoot in a vat of grapes with a local—and experienced—grape stomper. Another episode ends with Lucy being offered a Hollywood contract. But instead of being excited for Lucy, Ricky, Fred and Ethel insist they need to return to New York. She has to decide between staying and working in Hollywood and being with Little Ricky. She has no choice but to pass on this once-in-a-lifetime opportunity.

My mother had dreams of becoming an attorney or writer, but her life revolved around the day-to-day care of us five children. She was strong, intelligent and a voracious reader who took classes and went to lectures, but she never overcame the barriers, internal and external, to reaching her professional goals. In spite of this, Mom continually preached to all of us—sons and daughters—that the possibilities for our futures were limitless.

As an adult, I always worked outside the home, and pursued a range of interests and passions. And after I was married, with children, Mom and I often commiserated about those challenges. Connecting the dots between our lives and Lucy's gave us perspective and humor. Mom knew that Lucy could teach both of us a thing or two.

JOANNE DURKEE · PLEASANT HILL, CA

Dazzling the Guys at Fort Leonard Wood

Daniel J. Travanti bides his time before *Hill Street Blues*.

During the winter of 1963, as part of my three-year term in the Army, I was at Fort Leonard Wood, Missouri, in an advanced training course that was preparing me for my regular assignment. Most of the other troops there were in the National Guard, fulfilling their six-month active-duty requirements.

Daniel J. Travanti, who was from Kenosha, Wisconsin, was one of my colleagues. Travanti had already begun his acting career, having appeared in some stage productions. He hung out with several of us who were from Chicago. Weekends, we'd head to a nearby town to play pool and have a beer, always hoping to meet and dance with the local girls. After a few drinks, Travanti never passed up an opportunity to show off his acting skills. We always subjected him to a lot of razzing and negative comments when he did this. It didn't bother him—instead, he'd remind us that someday he would hit the big time, and we'd be asking him for an autograph. Of course, that day arrived and Dan became a successful actor!

In 1983, he replied to an inquiry of mine by sending a picture of himself on which he wrote: "To John, of course I remember that winter at Leonard Wood. Thanks for the reminder, and the nice words." He signed it "fellow guardsman." I was grateful that he didn't include "I told you so."

JOHN VRABEC · ALBUQUERQUE, NM

Travanti played Capt. Frank Furillo on the cop drama from 1981 to '87.

Alex Haley Talks Family

Author gives cordial interview over sweet potato pie.

———

When the Board of Education in Dayton, Ohio, hosted a fundraising dinner for its Head Start program in 1982, my wife, Virginia, and I went to see the featured speaker at the event, author Alex Haley. I was an editor in nearby Sidney. I met Haley months earlier after his keynote address at the California Writers Club. This time I hoped to interview him.

After Haley finished his speech at the fundraiser, I reminded him of our previous meeting. He invited us to his hotel room to talk. I was nervous about interviewing such an important writer, but he put me at ease. He offered us sweet potato pie and talked about his family, including his parents, Simon and Bertha, his brothers, George and Julius, and his many cousins.

We learned that his maternal grandmother, Cynthia, told him about a slave named Kunta Kinte and piqued his interest in learning about his family tree. Haley's extensive genealogical research going back seven generations led to his novel *Roots*.

"The story of Kunta Kinte is the story of all Black people whose ancestors were slaves," he said.

I remember my surprise that such a famous person as Haley would treat me as an equal. His manner toward us showed no hint that he held an esteemed position in the world of literature.

TOM MACH · LAWRENCE, KS

Tom met Alex Haley after attending lectures the author gave in California and Ohio.

Audience favorite Mary Martin was known for her warm interactions with fans.

Backstage with Mary Martin

Peter Pan actress tells fan to follow her dreams.

Mary Martin played the role of Peter Pan, the boy who never grew up, when the musical of that name opened on Broadway in 1954. I saw the spectacular production several months later when it was broadcast on NBC and my mother encouraged me to watch it on our new television. I was 10, and Mary's talent had me utterly convinced that she was a boy.

I began to write to her, and you can imagine my surprise when, after my fourth letter, I received a registered letter from her in return. After that, I continued to correspond with her, and she kept writing me back, telling me to follow my dreams. I began to wonder if I could meet this Broadway star!

In 1963, Mary performed at the Fisher Theatre in Detroit in *Hello, Dolly!* In one of her letters, she told me to come backstage after a show, and so I did. Later, I also got to go backstage at her shows in Cincinnati and New York.

For the remainder of her life, wherever she happened to be, Mary wrote to me. I still cherish those letters, which were caring and encouraging. Mary treated her audience with warmth and goodwill. She gave me confidence and treated me as a friend. She was so much more than a star.

MARY F. BURDICK · LEXINGTON, MI

BOB AND LUCY

These two bright stars together are comedy gold.

1963 »

Choice for Laughs

As the trailer for this movie says, "Where there's Hope there's laughter...and Lucy makes 'em louder!" The two play a married couple in *Critic's Choice.*

« 1960

Love Affair?

In *The Facts of Life* Bob Hope and Lucille Ball are not married, but are tempted to cheat on their spouses with each other. The film received one Oscar and four other nominations.

THAT'S ENTERTAINMENT!

HELLO AMERICA
Dave Garroway and his bride, Pamela Wilde, celebrate their nuptials on NBC's *Today* program in 1956. Garroway joined as host when the show debuted in 1952. His laid-back manner was a hit with viewers.

MOVE OVER, MR. MOONEY
Guest star Frankie Avalon entertains tellers at the local bank as Lucille Ball sings along in a still from Ball's second TV sitcom, "The Lucy Show," which debuted in 1962.

Gavin worked with two legendary directors in 1960: Stanley Kubrick and Alfred Hitchcock.

Celebrity Diplomat

John Gavin treats fans like VIPs.

John Gavin was Hollywood's next big thing in 1960. After seeing him in *Imitation of Life* the year before, my high-school-age sister, Susan, had written him a fan letter. Universal Studios sent her several 8-by-10-inch glossy photos and apparently kept her letter on file.

Gavin was in theaters as Janet Leigh's fiance in *Psycho* when he came to Indianapolis to promote three movies coming out in 1961, including *Tammy Tell Me True* with Sandra Dee. An agent invited Susan to a lunch with Gavin at the Lincoln Hotel. Susan managed to include our sister Nancy and me in the invitation.

A handful of people were at the luncheon, including a photographer. The 6-foot-4-inch Gavin looked like an Olympic god—anyone would know he was a movie star. He pulled out the chairs for Nancy and Susan, saying, "Let me seat the Sisters Woodworth." Such class! Gavin chatted warmly with us, telling us that his mother was of Hispanic origin and that he spoke fluent Spanish.

Fast-forward 27 years to 1987: Gavin was involved in politics, having served as ambassador to Mexico under President Ronald Reagan. Gavin was in Indianapolis for a lecture my mother and I attended. Afterward, I showed the former actor the photos of our 1960 meeting. I'm sure he had no recollection of that lunch, but he was gracious, chatting with me and signing one of my photos. Whatever his status in Hollywood, John Gavin was always a superstar to the Woodworth family.

MALCOLM WOODWORTH · INDIANAPOLIS, IN

The Path to *Shaft*

The coolest private eye on screen.

Just as *Shaft* (1971) revolutionized film, Richard Roundtree's role as John Shaft changed his life forever. It was the first Black action film and he was its hero— the smartest, toughest, coolest private eye in a sweet leather package. The franchise's first sequel, *Shaft's Big Score*, sealed the deal in 1972. Roundtree went on to more film, TV and stage roles, sharing credits with Laurence Olivier, Clint Eastwood, Peter O'Toole, Samuel L. Jackson, Morgan Freeman and Brad Pitt, among others.

Roundtree played football when he was young, and was on his high school's U.S.-ranked team in New Rochelle, New York. He won a scholarship to Southern Illinois University. He dreamed of going pro but changed his mind after suffering a couple of concussions.

Then he was a fashion model. He left college after Eunice Johnson of *Ebony* magazine asked him to model in the magazine's Fashion Fair. He invested in his new direction by taking acting lessons and then got some gigs, including with the Negro Ensemble Company's *The Great White Hope*.

Roundtree had the John Shaft look. He didn't even know what a screen test was when he got a call from legendary director Gordon Parks. Parks pointed to a pile of photos, saying that he wanted someone with that look. "And there's an ad there that I had done as a model," Roundtree told *The Boston Herald* in 2019. "I said, 'Mr. Parks, that's me.' And that was it."

He's talked about Blaxploitation. "Who's being exploited?" he asked *The New York Times* recently. "It gave a lot of people work. It gave a lot of people entree into the business, including a lot of our present-day producers and directors … I view it as a positive."

Roundtree also is a breast cancer survivor. He was diagnosed at age 51, undergoing both a mastectomy and chemotherapy. Fearing it would hurt his career, he kept his ailment and the treatment he received a secret for five years. Now he's an advocate for early detection.

Richard Roundtree was born in 1942.

AMY RABIDEAU SILVERS

No White Shoes
After Labor Day

Rule applies even if you're Terry Bradshaw.

The Pittsburgh Steelers were woeful for many years, and had just finished the 1969-'70 season at 1-13. In 1970, they won a coin toss—against the equally dismal Chicago Bears—that gave them the first selection in the NFL draft. The Steelers' pick, quarterback Terry Bradshaw, got a lot of publicity in the Pittsburgh media.

As football season was starting, I began working for the A.S. Beck Shoe Corp. in its men's store on Fifth Avenue in downtown Pittsburgh. A.S. Beck was a midpriced brand, in competition with the likes of Florsheim and Jarman.

The store manager usually was the person who approached customers, but he wasn't available the day a tall, blond young man came into the store. I recognized Bradshaw right away. The store was not very big and he didn't take long to look over the wall displays and racks of shoes. I asked him if I could be of assistance.

"Do you have any white shoes?" he asked.

I smiled and told him that he wouldn't find white shoes anywhere in Pittsburgh at that time of the year. White-shoe season was from Easter to Labor Day, so all of our white shoes had been shipped to the stores in Florida. He thanked me, left and walked to the Jarman store, where I'm sure he had the same conversation with a salesman.

JOE LIKAVEC · TELFORD, TN

Bradshaw led the Steelers to four Super Bowl titles in the '70s.

Jackie Robinson (1919-1972) once said, "A life is not important except in the impact it has on other lives."

Bringing About Change

Starting at first base for the Brooklyn Dodgers.

History took a bold turn on April 15, 1947, when Jackie Robinson put on a Brooklyn Dodgers uniform and broke baseball's color barrier. For the first time since 1889, Major League Baseball was officially integrated. Historians now consider this a watershed moment that influenced President Truman's order to integrate the armed forces the following year, with ripples to the civil rights movement and present day.

A gifted athlete, Robinson was the first to win varsity letters in four sports at UCLA: baseball, basketball, football and track.

While serving with the Army, 2nd Lt. Jack Robinson was arrested and faced court-martial in 1944 after refusing to move to the back of a segregated military bus. He won an honorable discharge more than a decade before Rosa Parks refused to move to the back of her bus.

Taking to the field, he joined the Negro League's Kansas City Monarchs in 1945, a star with a .387 batting average. The Dodgers' Branch Rickey saw Robinson as the right man to break the color barrier. Robinson was National League Rookie of the Year in 1947. In 1949, he became the league's Most Valuable Player, and in 1955, he helped Brooklyn win the World Series.

Robinson was an activist and was long involved in civil rights, including with the NAACP and as a speaker at the March on Washington in 1963.

He was also a businessman. He joined Chock full o' Nuts, the first Black vice president of a Fortune 500 firm. He co-founded Freedom National Bank of Harlem, and created the Jackie Robinson Construction Co. to build housing for low-income people.

Robinson was named to the Baseball Hall of Fame in 1962. His number was later retired across all MLB teams. The exception: All players can wear 42 on Jackie Robinson Day, usually April 15.

AMY RABIDEAU SILVERS

Shooting Star

Carrie Fisher blasts to fame as *Star Wars'* Princess Leia.

Long before Carrie Fisher became the female lead of the *Star Wars* universe in 1977, she was born into the rarified air of Hollywood royalty. Her parents, Debbie Reynolds and Eddie Fisher, were known as America's sweethearts before scandal ended the marriage. Carrie Fisher found her own kind of fame, best known, of course, for her role as Princess Leia Organa. And like her movie character, she learned to speak up, sharing the realities of her life with humor and grace.

Fisher actually hated those buns when filming *Star Wars*. "To put more hair on either side of a round face is going to make it even wider," Fisher said. "So that was my problem with that."

She dropped out of Beverly Hills High School in 1973, moving to England to study acting. She later attended Sarah Lawrence College before leaving to make the first *Star Wars*.

She was witty. Whatever the subject, Fisher could be wise, funny or both. Asked why Princess Leia never got her own lightsaber, Fisher noted: "Even in space, there's a double standard."

She was honest. Fisher was open about struggles in her life—including bipolar disorder and addiction—and the treatments she got. Her experience led her to advocate for people to get the help they need.

Fisher was the successful author of memoirs and autobiographical novels, including *Postcards from the Edge* (1987), later made into a movie with Meryl Streep and Shirley MacLaine. Fisher was also in demand as a script doctor, polishing story elements in *Sister Act* (1992) and a few of the *Star Wars* prequels.

She had a film life after death. Fisher died before her posthumous role in *The Rise of Skywalker*. Writer-director J.J. Abrams realized that unused footage

Carrie Fisher (1956-2016) said of her role in *Star Wars,* "I like Princess Leia. I like how she handles things ... she tells the truth."

from the original *Star Wars* could help bring Fisher back to finish Leia's story. "It was a bit like having a dozen pieces of a jigsaw puzzle and then having to make other pieces around it," Abrams said. "You couldn't tell the end of the Skywalker saga without Leia."

AMY RABIDEAU SILVERS

C-3PO Takes 5

Anthony Daniels, as robot C-3PO, relaxes against a padded board
while script supervisor Ann Skinner checks her notes during
the filming of *Star Wars* (1977) in Tunisia. The blockbuster film
launched a wildly successful 12-movie franchise.

CHAPTER 9

PLAY THAT MUSIC

Feel the rhythm of old songs playing in
your head while you review these accounts
of legendary musicians and more.

Hot-Rod Santa

Wouldn't it be nice if St. Nick drove a little deuce coupe?
The Beach Boys—Al Jardine, Dennis Wilson, Carl Wilson,
Mike Love and Brian Wilson as Santa—pose in 1963.

The King of Swing Plays Mozart

Benny Goodman makes dinner party dance.

M y husband, Jim, was principal clarinetist in the Tucson Symphony Orchestra when Benny Goodman was a guest soloist with the orchestra in October 1960. Goodman performed "Clarinet Concerto in A Major" (Mozart) and "Concertino for Clarinet" (Weber).

Goodman asked Jim to organize a jazz ensemble for a swing music encore. Partway through the 30-minute encore, Benny introduced Jim as his "friend who plays beautiful clarinet in the orchestra and also plays jazz." Jim remembered feeling as if he was walking on air as he went onstage to play "Moonglow." By the second chorus, Goodman had the audience clapping to the beat—then he joined in playing with Jim. The audience didn't want it to end.

While Goodman was in Tucson, we gave him a small dinner party. He was charming and interesting, and put us at ease. He brought his clarinet, and after dinner he, Jim and Sam—a professor of clarinet at the University of Arizona—played trio selections in our living room. Goodman even invited our son Jimmy, 15 and also a clarinetist, to join them. At Goodman's request, Gary, our 11-year-old, the first chair clarinetist in the Tucson Youth Symphony, played for him, too. Heady stuff!

JEANNE PAFFORD GLASGOW · AUSTIN, TX

Benny Goodman, left, enjoys a pre-dinner drink with host Jim Glasgow in 1960.

Shirley Jones sang "Till There Was You" in the film version of *The Music Man.*

Never Till Now

Musical bell rings true for the first time.

———

When I first met my wife, Jane, we were listening to Beatles' music at a school reunion. Then someone changed the CD player to play random selections by various artists. So Jane and I talked about how the Beatles were the best ever. We decided to go together the next week to a club that played only the Beatles.

We danced to fast and slow tunes. But our favorite slow tune was the Beatles' recording of "Till There Was You," a beautiful song written by Meredith Willson and first performed by Barbara Cook and Robert Preston in the 1957 Broadway hit *The Music Man*. Shirley Jones sang it with Preston in the 1962 movie.

Jane and I went back to the club every week, hoping each time they'd play our favorite song.

"There were bells on a hill/ But I never heard them ringing/ No, I never heard them at all/ Till there was you."

That was—and is—very true for me, from when we started dating to today. Everything around me seemed more positive.

"Then there was music and wonderful roses/ They tell me in sweet fragrant meadows/ Of dawn and dew/ There was love all around/ but I never heard it singing/ No, I never heard it at all/ Till there was you."

It is astonishing how just putting your song on the turntable can make you feel as though you are the only two people in the world at that very moment.

STEVE MELTON · DALLAS, TX

Doris Day made "Tea for Two" a sweet ballad in the 1950 film of the same name.

Silly One Sticks

Little ditty about tea serves up lifetime of laughs.

Jack and I had the stupidest song. We met on a blind date in 1952. He was a Marine stationed in Santa Ana, California, and on his way to Korea. I had just graduated from high school. We were apart more than we were together the next two years.

When he was discharged, Jack went home to Columbus, Ohio, for a few months, until he returned to Los Angeles for our wedding.

Where was I all that time? Living at home, listening to romantic songs by singers such as Jo Stafford ("You Belong to Me"), Eddie Fisher ("Wish You Were Here") and Perry Como ("No Other Love"). I wrote to Jack almost every night, putting purple 3-cent stamps on the front of the envelopes and writing SWAK—sealed with a kiss—on the back, while I played Jackie Gleason's album *Music For Lovers Only*.

Yet somehow—neither of us knows exactly how—we adopted "Tea for Two" as our song. We didn't even drink tea. In fact, Jack and I never drank the same beverages. He liked coffee or beer; I preferred milk or soda.

"We will raise a family, a boy for you, and a girl for me/ Oh, can't you see how happy we would be?" We had to change those lyrics eventually—we had three boys and five girls.

We have laughed about this through the years. What a ridiculous song!

JOANN SCHUELLER COOKE · PRESCOTT, AZ

They're Playing Our Song

A sweet tune and a few words bring back love's lyrical early days.

GOLDEN MOMENT

On Dec. 7, 1946, I went on a date and found my soul mate. I knew she was the right one, so 10 days later, I asked Gerry to marry me. Our wedding was the following August. At one point when we were dating, Gerry performed the Peggy Lee song "Golden Earrings" at an amateur show. She was the only girl there, as far as I was concerned. It was our song until she passed away in 1998. Today, when my granddaughters sing it for me, it brings tears to my eyes.

STANLEY BROWN
ANGOLA, NY

....

RIGHTEOUS MEMORIES

My husband, Lynn, and I met in 1956, when we were both still in high school. We lived 25 miles apart. Lynn worked on his parents' farm, but on Saturdays and Sundays he'd finish early and drive to my house. We'd go to a movie or just drive around, talking and listening to the radio. The first time we heard Gene Vincent sing "Unchained Melody" we knew it was our song. It described how we felt when we were apart.

We married the next year. When the version by the Righteous Brothers, right, was released in 1965, it became our favorite.

SHARON TURNER
ARLINGTON, IN

BLUE SEAS, BLUE EYES

When I was a high school senior, the students picked "Harbor Lights" as the class song. Later, at our wedding, David and I danced to "Harbor Lights" for the first time as husband and wife. He held me close as I looked into his beautiful blue eyes.

After that moment, whenever "Harbor Lights" played on the radio, we were reminded of how our love had grown through the years. Though David died in 2019, I still see his blue eyes, especially when I hear our song.

HELEN TRUITT
LEWES, DE

GUESSING GAME

Scott was my first crush when I was 14 and he was 17. We reconnected on Facebook 30 years later. I'd post song lyrics and ask friends to guess the song and artist. Scott always played along. We chatted on Facebook for a few months, but he hadn't asked me out. So I posted the lyrics to "I'd Really Love to See You Tonight," which was a hit for England Dan and John Ford Coley in 1976. When Scott guessed correctly, I replied "You do?!"

We married in 2012.

MELISSA SNOOKS PATE
SOLSBERRY, IN

The Righteous Brothers smile for the camera circa 1970.

She Told Him So

The Dixie Cups were right after all.

———

Dan and I started dating in the spring of 1964. In early 1965, he gave me a single of the hit "Chapel of Love." My brother wasn't too happy about it, but I told him, "One day Dan and I are going to get married."

After I graduated from high school in June 1965, I was headed to New York to stay with a friend and her family. Dan drove me to the train station, and we decided at that point to date other people while we were apart.

We got back together when I returned home to Michigan. In 1966, The Happenings' version of "See You in September" was a big hit. That song became another favorite for Dan and me, perhaps because it described what had happened in our relationship.

"Here we are/ Saying goodbye at the station/ Summer vacation/ Is taking you away."

We married in October 1967; I knew we would share a long journey together. We raised two sons, who are now music teachers and accomplished jazz musicians.

Both "Chapel of Love" and "See You in September" bring a smile to our faces every time we hear them. We stop and just listen to the words that brought us together.

ROBERTA BARASZU · KENNESAW, GA

The Dixie Cups hit No. 1 on the pop chart in 1964 with "Chapel of Love."

"At Last" made Etta James a vocal legend.

It Took a While

Longtime friends discover romance in retirement.

M y wife, Barbara, and I first met when we both started teaching at the same high school in September 1968. We were on that staff for 16 years, and many of those years we worked together as senior class advisers.

Barbara left the school in 1984 to work as an administrator in a different district. I worked the rest of my 32-year career in my original school district.

We didn't meet again until 2008, when we both attended a luncheon for teacher retirees. We were both in our mid 60s and each of us had always been single. We began dating.

We married in 2011. The priest who officiated at our wedding said Barbara and I were the oldest couple that he had ever married for the first time. To almost everyone who knew us, it seemed plain that neither of us would ever marry.

When we entered the reception room, the DJ played Etta James' version of "At Last." The song started as the door opened and we walked in just as Etta sang "At La-a-a-st!" Our guests responded with riotous laughter and applause.

It's been our song ever since.

GENE AMARAL · UNION CITY, CA

Ella Fitzgerald was the most popular female jazz singer of her generation.

Exclusive with Ella Fitzgerald

Meeting with famous personality has a bumpy start.

Jazz singer Ella Fitzgerald came to Wilmington, North Carolina, in the mid 1980s when I was a young TV reporter. I'd received a tip about what time her flight was arriving, so I went to the airport to meet her.

Fitzgerald was traveling alone and thus didn't have any handlers or public relations people with her. I greeted her and asked for an interview, to which she agreed. We arranged to meet at the Hilton Hotel downtown.

Excited to score this exclusive talk with the legendary performer, I got to the hotel ahead of time. I was a "one-man band" and set up my own camera and lights. When she arrived, I coaxed her to sit down for the interview in the hotel lobby, and got her lavalier microphone in place.

I almost blew my big chance with my first question, asking what it was like, being such a great musician for so many years.

She exclaimed in exasperation, "You reporters are always reminding me of how old I am!" She reached to remove her mic and began to stand to leave. I quickly apologized.

What a relief that we went on to have a beautiful interview. I learned my lesson, and after that, I was more sensitive in my conversations with famous entertainers.

JEFF WEISER · SCARSDALE, NY

ELVIS ON FILM

Who could resist the King?

MGM Presents
ELVIS PRESLEY
AT HIS GREATEST
Jailhouse Rock

1957 »

Party at the County Jail?
Elvis Presley makes an instant classic when he stars, shaking his hips, in musical drama *Jailhouse Rock*.

ELVIS PRESLEY
...SINGIN' MAN!
...FIGHTIN' MAN!
...LOVIN' MAN!

RICHARD **EGAN**
DEBRA **PAGET**
AND INTRODUCING ELVIS **PRESLEY**

LOVE ME TENDER

A 20th CENTURY-FOX CINEMASCOPE PICTURE

Directed by DAVID WEISBART · ROBERT D. WEBB

HEAR MR. ROCK 'n' ROLL SING
"Love Me Tender"
"We're Gonna Move"
"Poor Boy"
"Let Me"

« 1956

Action and Romance
Mr. Rock 'n' Roll himself gets caught up, as this movie poster claims, being a singin', fightin' and lovin' man in *Love Me Tender*.

MUSIC GREATS

ROYAL VISIT
President Richard M. Nixon poses with Elvis Presley in the White House in 1970. Elvis asked for—and received—a federal narcotics agent's badge at that meeting. The King, in turn, tried to give the president a Colt .45, but the Secret Service confiscated it.

KING OF SOUL
Singer Otis Redding performs in 1967. The 26-year-old writer of "Respect" and other iconic hits died that December when his new private jet went down in a lake near Madison, Wisconsin.

IN MEMORIAM
Fans of Elvis Presley gather at the gates of Graceland, his home in Memphis, Tennessee, a few days after his death on Aug. 16, 1977.

Paul's smooch capped Connie's thrilling evening out with friends.

An Evening with Crooner Paul Anka

Teen idol meets fans face to face.

M y sister Connie is several years older than me. After she graduated from high school, she worked at I-T-E Electric Circuit Breaker Co. in Greensburg, Pennsylvania, in the early 1960s. The office was abuzz one day with talk of Paul Anka's upcoming show at the Holiday Inn in Monroeville, just 30 minutes away. Paul was young and handsome and had a voice to melt a young woman's heart—Connie wasn't about to miss it.

The show started with dinner, then Paul sang many of their favorites, such as "Puppy Love" and "Lonely Boy." After the performance ended, Connie and her friends saw Paul walking down a hallway. They tried to catch up with him, but he went into his room, leaving a crowd of girls staring at the door.

A man came out and told them Mr. Anka would talk with them after he changed his clothes.

The girls went back to their tables to wait—Paul was supposed to be out in 15 minutes, but the girls waited for what seemed like an hour. Just as they began to worry they'd fallen for a ploy to let him escape, he reentered the room. A photographer was with him for anyone who wanted their picture taken with the star.

Connie didn't hesitate—in one of her photos with Paul, he even gave her a peck on the cheek. She came home so excited about that smooch!

Today my sister lives in a nursing home, but she's never forgotten the joy she felt in this picture.

RUTH ISHMAN · WINTER GARDEN, FL

Visionary Guitarist Les Paul

Leaving his mark in more ways than one.

L es Paul's solid-body electric guitar hit the market in 1952, decades after he began to experiment with a new sound. Made by Gibson, the guitar found a following from across the musical spectrum that included jazz master Al Di Meola and hard rocker Jimmy Page of Led Zeppelin. Paul's influence on studio technology may be greater: He invented overdubbing, multitrack recording and other techniques that ushered in the era of modern music. "He made technology a musical instrument," said producer and record executive Don Was. "We're all deeply in his debt."

Lester William Polsfuss' piano teacher wasn't impressed, sending home a note: "Your boy Lester will never learn music, so save your money." Young Les, undeterred, formed his own orchestra by age 10 and then took up guitar and electronics.

He was a pop star. Paul and his wife, Mary Ford, had dozens of Top 40 tunes, and scored a No. 1 hit with "How High The Moon" in 1951, which used overdubbing and other of his innovations. On TV, they hosted *Les Paul and Mary Ford at Home* from 1952 to '54.

Paul didn't let a bad break end his career. After a car crash shattered his right arm and elbow in 1948, he convinced doctors to set the arm in the "guitar-picking and cradling position."

He called his first solid-body model— built of pine blocks and guitar parts— The Log. And Paul loved playing. He performed country and pop and finally settled into weekly jazz gigs. "I probably will play until I fall over," he said in 2005. He kept playing until just months before his death at 94.

The "Number One" Gibson Goldtop, owned and modified by Paul, sold at auction for $930,000 in 2021.

He was a true Halls of Famer. Les Paul (1915-2009) remains the only person inducted into the Rock and Roll Hall of Fame and National Inventors Hall of Fame. He also won multiple Grammys and was awarded the National Medal of Arts.

"I didn't know it was going to change the world, but I knew it was going to make some noise," said Les Paul on his guitar.

AMY RABIDEAU SILVERS

Rockabilly

"Go, boy, go," became the groovier, "Go, cat, go."

W hat else would you call a rocked-up version of hillbilly music? The new sound of country songs played with a driving rhythm and blues style burst out of the South in the mid-1950s. At Sun Studios in Memphis, Tennessee, producer Sam Phillips engineered a "slap-back" echo effect that added to rockabilly's distinctive twang. The 1956 hit "Blue Suede Shoes" by rockabilly pioneer Carl Perkins—recorded a few months later by none other than Elvis Presley—made this early form of rock 'n' roll a national sensation.

NATALIE WYSONG

Carl Perkins credited John Westbrook, a Black man who worked alongside Perkins' father as a sharecropper, with teaching him blues guitar.

David Bowie's Ziggy Stardust persona defined the campy theatricality of glitter rock. Bowie retired the hugely popular alter ego after only a year.

GLITTER ROCK

ALSO KNOWN AS "GLAM ROCK" IN THE U.K., WHERE it started, this pop culture movement was a sharp turn away from '60s hippie influence and a protest against mainstream rock 'n' roll. Highly produced concerts—often themed with space-age futurism—celebrated synthetic excess, with artists in heavy makeup, glitzy bodysuits and sky-high platform shoes. Merriam-Webster added the term in 1972, the year Roxy Music and David Bowie released bestselling albums—proof that rock music was still pushing limits.

NATALIE WYSONG

MAKING OF A NAME

Born David Jones, the musician told an interviewer he picked the edgier "Bowie" as a tribute to 19th-century American folk hero Jim Bowie.

Jazz VIP in the Audience

Nat Adderley won't say no to some Hank Williams songs.

A country and gospel singer and guitar picker, I try to bring a little sunshine into people's lives by giving mini concerts in patients' rooms at hospitals and assisted living facilities.

Years ago, I was performing at a facility in Lakeland, Florida. I passed one room and noticed a man talking on the phone, so I went on by. The resident next door had visitors, and when I finished my performance for them, one of the visitors said I should go back and sing for that man next door.

He was no longer talking on the phone, so I walked in and said, "You sure look like you need to be sung to!"

"I sure do," he said.

I asked him if he liked the music of Hank Williams Sr.

"Oh yes," he said. "I met him several months before he died."

I sang two or three Hank Williams songs, and then the man's phone rang again. I finished up and left, all without learning his name.

A week later, a Lakeland newspaper ran a front-page article with a picture of the man I'd played for. He was Nat Adderley, brother of jazz great Julian "Cannonball" Adderley, and a jazz legend in his own right. My encounter with him was brief, but of course I never forgot it.

KEITH MARR · PLANT CITY, FL

The jazz classic "Work Song" is one of songwriter Nat Adderley's most recognizable numbers.

LEFT: MICHAEL OCHS ARCHIVES/GETTY IMAGES

Elvis Has Entered the Building

He's in the multipurpose room.

___

When I was a teenager back in the 1950s, I started collecting Elvis' records—singles and LPs.

My son, Scott, grew up to be a huge fan too. From the time he was young, Scott borrowed all my records.

In 1975, when he was 10, Woodcrest Elementary School in Port Neches, Texas, held a talent contest. Scott wanted to perform as Elvis, but he didn't have a costume. So while he was at school, I tailored one of my satin blouses, cutting it down to fit Scott and adding rows of red and silver sequins. I also bought him white shoes and jeans. Scott tried on the outfit as soon as he got home, then grabbed his guitar and put on a record. He was off in his own world.

The morning of the talent contest, he was so excited he couldn't finish his breakfast. When he walked in after school, he had a huge smile.

"Thank you, thank you very much," he said, in his best deep Elvis voice.

Then he told me about his day. "Mama, it was crazy. The girls screamed so loud I don't think anyone heard the music. They followed me around school. On my way home I had to take a shortcut so I could lose a couple of girls that were following me."

Scott won the talent show, and after that, he dressed up in the Elvis costume whenever he had the chance. And we both still love to listen to our Elvis records.

DEANNA DUNLAP · GROVES, TX

The Cool Kids

The Rolling Stones—Mick Jagger, Bill Wyman, Brian Jones, Keith Richards and Charlie Watts—in a rare quiet moment in their early days.